Newbery Authors
of the
Eastern Seaboard

Newbery Authors
of the
Eastern Seaboard

Integrating Social Studies and Literature, Grades 5-8

Joanne Kelly

Photographs by
Charles Kelly

Drawings and Maps by
Pat Martin

1994
Teacher Ideas Press
A Division of
Libraries Unlimited, Inc.
Englewood, Colorado

In Memory of My Mother

TEACHER IDEAS PRESS
A Division of
Libraries Unlimited, Inc.
P.O. Box 6633
Englewood, CO 80155-6633
1-800-237-6124

Project Editor: Kevin W. Perizzolo
Copy Editor: Tama Serfoss
Proofreader: Jason Cook
Interior Book Design and Typesetting: Judy Gay Matthews

Library of Congress Cataloging-in-Publication Data

Kelly, Joanne, 1934-
    Newbery authors of the Eastern Seaboard : integrating social studies and literature, grades 5-8 / Joanne Kelly ; photographs by Charles Kelly ; drawings and maps by Pat Martin.
    ix, 159 p. 22x28 cm.
    Includes bibliographical references and index.
    ISBN 1-56308-122-9
    1. Social sciences--Study and teaching (Elementary)--United States. 2. Children's literature--Study and teaching (Elementary)--United States. 3. Children's stories, American. I. Title.
LB1584.K37 1994
372.83--dc20   94-19529
                                                                                          CIP

Contents

Acknowledgments

Gathering the material for this book was made far easier by several talented librarians who have shared my interest and enthusiasm. My sincere thanks go to my friends, librarian Laurel Goodgion of Newington, Connecticut, and Marie Catudal of Crisfield, Maryland. Thanks also to Janice Harrington and the other fine librarians of the Champaign Public Library, Champaign, Illinois, who patiently endured my millions of interlibrary loan requests.

Introduction

Many years ago, when my two sons were still young, our family shared the hilarious misadventures of a raccoon named Rascal and the poignant story of a boy named Sterling. While vacationing in Wisconsin we decided to try to locate the setting of the story, Sterling North's house in Edgerton, using the descriptions of places given in the book. Sterling North proved to be an accurate guide, and we were thrilled to find the house just where it should have been, near the church. In those days there was no sign to correctly identify our find, but there could be no mistaking it.

"Look! There's the bay window where Sterling put the Christmas tree!"

"Mom! There's Poe's steeple!"

"Gosh! I'll bet that's the very tree where Sterling built his hideaway."

That thrilling experience and the new perspective it gave us about the book and the area were not forgotten. As an elementary school librarian I continued to investigate the possibilities of making the settings of good books come to life for my students. The school children and I visited locations within a reasonable distance and wrote to those farther away, requesting information.

Children have always been excited about discovering how "the real place" actually looks, how it differs from the story setting, and how the author incorporated local features and history into the plot. Would it be possible to really go there, and what would you find if you did?

With some encouragement, children can use this information to increase their knowledge of the world around them by investigating the geography of the literary setting and area. The possibilities for learning and for stimulating thinking skills are endless; however, care should be taken not to destroy a child's pleasure in the story itself. The activities suggested here should be shaped to fit the individual needs of students or adapted for the framework of the local curriculum.

The 13 books presented here span a broad range of reading levels. They are arranged progressively by the maturity of the intended reader; certainly there is some overlapping, and certainly this sequencing is arguable. Have fun with this book, and have a great time introducing children to the real places.

1

Chincoteague and
Assateague Islands, Virginia

The Settings for Marguerite Henry's

Misty of Chincoteague
Rand McNally, 1947. 172 pages.

Sea Star: Orphan of Chincoteague
Rand McNally, 1949. 172 pages.

Stormy, Misty's Foal
Rand McNally, 1963. 224 pages.

Misty's Twilight
Macmillan, 1992. 143 pages.

Book Summaries

Misty of Chincoteague

Legend has it that the ponies running wild on Assateague Island are the descendants of Moorish ponies that survived the shipwreck of a Spanish galleon off the Virginia coast. Paul and Maureen Beebe have set their sights on buying one of those ponies when the annual Pony Penning Day arrives. On that day, the ponies are rounded up and forced to swim to nearby Chincoteague Island where some of them are sold to benefit the volunteer fire department. Paul and Maureen live with their grandparents on a pony farm at the tip of Chincoteague Island, where they help with the care of the wild ponies that their grandfather purchases and readies for sale. Now they want a pony of their own, one that will never be sold to strangers and taken away.

But Paul and Maureen don't want just any pony. They are determined to buy the elusive Phantom, a filly who has outsmarted the roundup riders and eluded capture for the past two years. The children work for months earning the $100 they estimate they'll need to buy the Phantom, and Paul has finally reached the age where he will be able to ride in the roundup on Assateague. He is determined to bring in the Phantom.

When he is left alone to find the strays separated from the main herd, Paul discovers the Phantom and her new foal hiding in the woods. He is able to drive them to the area where the rest of the herd has been gathered and watches carefully while the horses are driven into the water for the short swim to Chincoteague. When it appears that the foal, whom Paul has named Misty, is too tiny to make the crossing, Paul dives into the water to help her to safety.

The children are bitterly disappointed when it seems that the Phantom and her foal have been sold before they have had a chance to bid on them. But the next day, the new owner and his son win another pony in the raffle, and they decide they don't want three horses. Paul and Maureen are finally able to buy the horse of their dreams and her beautiful little foal as well.

The children spend a happy year gentling and training the ponies, but it is clear that the Phantom often misses her life of freedom on Assateague. As the next Pony Penning Day approaches, the fire chief suggests that the Phantom be entered in the annual horse race because she seems to be the only Island pony with a chance to beat the perennial champion, Black Comet, from the mainland. Paul and Maureen have long been anticipating the race, hoping that the Phantom could run; now they spend all their time training her for the event.

Though Black Comet is the heavy favorite, island loyalties lie with the Phantom, and she is greeted with cheers from the spectators as she enters the track. Paul is the jockey. In a close and exciting race, he rides to victory.

Shortly after the race, the Phantom grows increasingly restless, so Paul and Maureen ride her along the shoreline. A wild stallion, Pied Piper, swims across the water from Assateague and bugles for the Phantom to join him. With hardly a moment's indecision, Paul allows the Phantom to follow the stallion back to freedom on Assateague. While the children will miss their horse, they are more than content to care for and love her wonderful foal, Misty.

Misty won the Lewis Carroll Shelf Award in 1961 and was named a Newbery Honor Book in 1948.

Sea Star: Orphan of Chincoteague

Paul and Maureen are playing with Misty in the meadows of the Pony Ranch when a small airplane unexpectedly lands on the grass. Two men in business suits emerge and introduce themselves to the children, explaining that they want to make a moving picture about the wild ponies of Assateague and want to buy Misty to use her in the picture. The children are horrified at the prospect of losing their pony and are gratified when Grandpa won't consider the idea. The men will stay and do filming of Pony Penning Day, however, and the Beebes offer to help them.

Business has not been prospering on the pony ranch and money is scarce. When Grandma goes to Richmond to enroll son Clarence Lee in college, she discovers the tuition, which must be paid in advance, is more than they can afford. Paul and Maureen quickly agree to sell Misty to the movie producers to pay for Clarence Lee's college education. Their offer is gratefully accepted by Grandma and Grandpa.

Preparations for Pony Penning Day continue, and Paul and Maureen are caught up in the hectic excitement, helping them avoid thinking about the day when Misty will leave them. Paul agrees to act as a guide for the movie production and leads the photographer to Tom's Cove to shoot the action of the roundup. The next day, he enters the bronc-busting contest at the Pony Penning Grounds. Paul rides the wild pony, Red Demon, for a terrifying 30 seconds and wins the top prize of 10 dollars.

The family builds a safe and comfortable crate for Misty's journey to New York, but the final parting is hard for everyone. Grandma sends Paul and Maureen to gather oysters on Assateague Island to keep their minds off their sorrow.

In Tom's Cove they make a grisly discovery: an old mare has died and birds are trying to swoop down on it. The scavengers are being fought off by a tiny foal, the dead horse's orphan. The children manage to capture the foal and bring it back to Chincoteague. They name him Sea Star and make arrangements to buy him from the fire department (which owns all the wild horses on Assateague) for the $10 Paul won.

The lonely foal has not been weaned and refuses to eat the mash that Paul has prepared. Grandpa insists that bottle feeding Sea Star will only cause him to grow up "ornery." The children fear the unhappy little horse will die, so they devise a desperate plan to save him.

A wild mare was injured during the Pony Penning Roundup and is being boarded at a local stable until she is healed. She had a nursing foal that was sold. She would be able to nurse Sea Star, but mares rarely accept foals that are not their own. Because mares recognize their foals by smell, the children think they can make the mare believe Sea Star is her own foal by giving both horses the same smell. They rub the foal and the horse with strongly scented myrtle leaves and then introduce them to each other. To everyone's joy, the mare allows the foal to suckle after a few breath-taking moments. The mare comes to live on the Beebe pony ranch until Sea Star is grown enough to be on his own.

Stormy, Misty's Foal

Misty is back at home on the Pony Ranch, expecting her first foal. Paul and Maureen are in a frenzy of anticipation and concern. The publicity from the book and film about Misty have helped bring prosperity to the ranch, and Grandpa's herd has increased enough that most of the horses are kept in winter pasture on the north end of the island. The news of Misty's expected baby has increased public interest in her and in the islands of Chincoteague and Assateague. Children everywhere, it seems, are anxiously waiting.

An unseasonably severe storm suddenly hits the islands, causing electrical service to fail and the tides to rise to unprecedented levels. The Beebes make provisions to protect their livestock, including Misty, should the high water endanger them.

But the storm continues to grow, causing tremendous flooding all over the islands. Homes and businesses are in ruins, and the number of casualties among the wild and domestic animals is frightening. Grandpa is frantic about the safety of his herd on the northern tip of the island, and everyone on Chincoteague fears the worst for the wild ponies on Assateague.

The decision is made to evacuate all the residents of Chincoteague to nearby Wallops Island. Not only is the flood a threat, but there is also the danger of a typhoid epidemic caused by the large number of animal carcasses rotting on both islands. Helicopters arrive to carry out the evacuation.

Faced with the prospect of leaving Misty to have her foal alone, the Beebes turn the kitchen of their house into a temporary stable with hay on the floor and water in the sink. Here they hope she'll have the best chance of staying warm and dry. The other horses still at the ranch are led into the stables where the floors have been covered with bales of hay.

With heavy hearts, the family boards a helicopter for the flight to the evacuation center. Paul and Grandpa join other volunteers who begin searching the island for casualties. They hurry to the Pony Ranch and find Misty in good condition but with no new baby yet. Things are much worse for the rest of Grandpa's herd. Nearly all his ponies at the north end of the island have drowned.

On the fourth day of the storm, Grandpa decides to move Misty to a veterinarian's stable on the mainland where she will have her baby in safety. Late that night the whole family returns to their home on Chincoteague. As the storm begins to subside, the Beebe's begin the massive cleanup at the ranch while volunteers and disaster crews try to remove the rubble from the town and assess the damage to the wild pony herds. Grandpa works with the crews on Assateague and learns that only a fraction of the wild ponies survived the storm.

Soon, word comes that Misty has a new foal and both mother and daughter are in fine shape. The islanders all rejoice with the Beebe family; the happy news seems to be the one bright spot in their lives at the moment. As word of the foal born in the midst of disaster is carried on news broadcasts, congratulations come pouring in from across the nation.

The toll taken by the storm has been devastating, and it is decided to cancel Pony Penning until the wild herds on Assateague can be rebuilt. A plan to purchase recently sold horses is suggested but is dismissed as too expensive.

The producers of Misty's movie agree to hold benefit showings of the film with proceeds going to restocking the wild herds. A national Misty Disaster Fund is established and contributions from children soon begin to arrive with suggestions for names for the new filly. Everyone agrees that one of those suggestions, Stormy, is perfect. Paul and Maureen allow Misty and her baby to make personal appearances at theaters. Misty and Stormy make an exciting first appearance at a theater in Richmond, Virginia, and a new career seems launched for the famous pony.

In an epilogue, the author tells of the success of the fund-raising drive and the continuation of the Pony Penning tradition on Chincoteague.

Misty's Twilight

All her life, Sandy Price has dreamed of owning a Chincoteague pony. Now she is a mother with a young son and daughter, a physician with a successful practice, and has a horse farm all her own near Ocala, Florida. Now she can make her dream come true.

With her children, Pam and Chris, Sandy travels to Chincoteague for Pony Penning Day and is swept away with excitement and enthusiasm. They see all the sights on the island and watch the ponies swim from Assateague. They visit the Chincoteague Pony Ranch to see Misty's descendants and there she discovers Sunshine, Misty's great-granddaughter.

Sunshine and three other Chincoteague ponies return to the Florida horse farm with Sandy and, some time later, Sunshine is bred to a handsome thoroughbred. When her filly is born, Sandy names her Twilight and is sure that the foal is an exceptional pony.

Twilight doesn't disappoint her owner; she is intelligent, spirited, and beautiful. She readily learns to be a cutting horse, but she is at a disadvantage because of her size and unusual lineage. Next, she is trained to be a jumper and takes to the schooling with zest and clear talent. A foot injury however, keeps her from ever competing in that sport.

Finally, Sandy arranges to send Twilight, by now registered as "Misty's Twilight," to a school for dressage where her talents are successfully cultivated in preparation for an Olympic trial in 1996.

About the Author

Marguerite Breithaupt was born in Milwaukee, Wisconsin, in 1902, the youngest of five children. Her father owned a publishing business. At age seven, when she received a writing table outfitted with pencils, paper, scissors, paste, paper clips, and a pencil sharpener, Marguerite knew she wanted to be a writer. A year later, she sold her first story to *Deliniator* magazine for $12, and launched her career.

Marguerite continued writing through school, and she read constantly. After school and on Saturdays, she worked at the public library, mending books. Later she attended the Milwaukee State Teachers College and the University of Wisconsin-Milwaukee.

In 1923, Marguerite married Sidney Crocker Henry, a sales manager, who encouraged her to continue writing as they settled down in Chicago. She published articles in several national magazines. In 1939 they moved to two acres of land in Wayne, Illinois, west of Chicago. There Marguerite began writing books for children, publishing her first, *Auno and Tauno: A Story of Finland,* in 1940. There followed a number of nonfiction books, primarily in the Pictured Geography series for the Albert Whitman Company.

Justin Morgan Had a Horse, published in 1945, was the first Henry book illustrated by Wesley Dennis, beginning a long and successful collaboration. It was a Junior Literary Guild Selection, a Junior Scholastic Gold Seal Award, and a Newbery Honor book in 1946.

Her editors at Rand McNally suggested to Marguerite and Wesley Dennis to go to Chincoteague Island to see the wild pony roundup and perhaps do a book. There she met Clarence Beebe, owner of a local pony farm, and his grandchildren, Paul and Maureen. She also found a tiny cream-and-gold filly whom she loved instantly and named Misty. The filly was purchased from Beebe and, after several months, was shipped to the Henrys' land in Wayne. Marguerite began to write a story about her immediately. *Misty of Chincoteague*, published in 1947, was selected as a Newbery Honor Book in 1948 and the Lewis Carroll Shelf Award in 1961. Henry's *King of the Wind* (1948) won the Newbery Award in 1949.

Henry's most successful books have been a blending of fact and imagination. A *Sunset* magazine article on the Grand Canyon and a wild burro named Bright Angel touched off the research for *Brighty of the Grand Canyon* (1953). A trip to the Middle East in 1965 inspired *White Stallion of Lipizza* (1964), and *Gaudenzia, Pride of the Palio* (1960). Marguerite Henry is credited with being the first author to bring a body of horse stories to younger readers, but she has also written well-received informational books such as *Album of Horses* (1951), *Dear Readers and Riders* (1969), *All About Horses* (1962), and *Wagging Tails: An Album of Dogs* (1955), all published by Rand McNally.

Misty was returned to the Beebes on Chincoteague where she had many foals over the years. She made personal appearances all over the United States with her foal, Stormy. She died in 1972 at the age of 26, but her offspring provided Henry with inspiration for more novels culminating with *Misty's Twilight*, published in 1992 by Macmillan.

To date, Marguerite Henry has written 30 fiction and 23 nonfiction books. She was awarded the Children's Reading Round Table Award in 1961 and the Kerlin Award in 1975 for her work. Widowed in 1987, she lives and works in southern California.

Setting: Assateague and Chincoteague Islands, Virginia

Figure 1.1. Delmarva peninsula with Assateague and Chincoteague Islands.

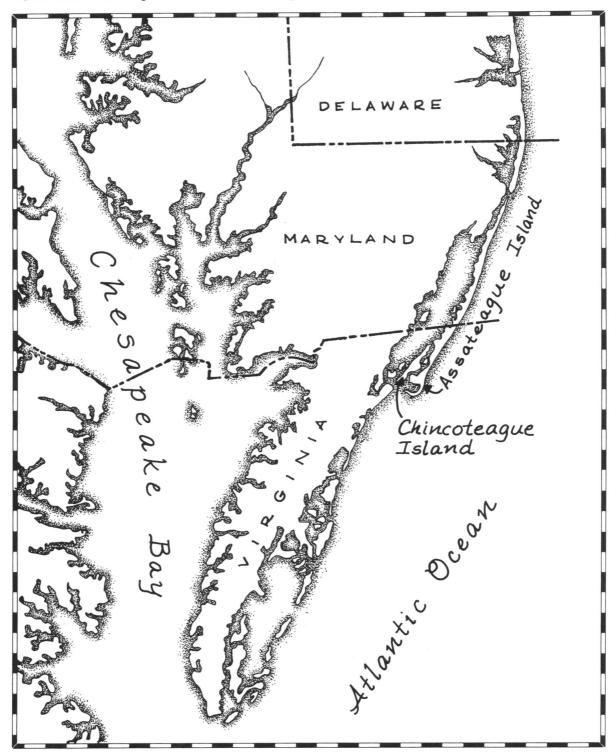

Just as described by Marguerite Henry, the barrier islands of Chincoteague and Assateague lie along the Atlantic coastline of Maryland and Virginia (see fig. 1.1). Chincoteague (see map A in the extended activities) is the inner island and lies completely within the state of Virginia. It is 7 miles long, 1.5 miles wide, and has a population of about 3,500 people. It is protected from the Atlantic Ocean by Assateague Island to the east, but the two are separated only by the narrow, marshy Chincoteague Channel.

Assateague is 37 miles long and lies in both Maryland and Virginia. The entire island is protected, with Maryland's Assateague State Park covering the northern two-thirds of the island and the Chincoteague National Wildlife Refuge covering the southern third.

Local Native Americans knew the inner island as "Chincoteague" or "Beautiful Land Across the Water." The first land patent was issued in 1671 when Chincoteague was used as livestock range for settlers in Maryland. The island was largely uninhabited until the mid-nineteenth century when about 100 families lived there, raising cattle and horses. By 1857, there were nearly 1000 inhabitants on the tiny island, with a post office and a school. In 1861, when the rest of Virginia joined the Confederacy, Chincoteague pledged allegiance to the Union and maintained sea trade with the north.

Today, seafood is the leading industry on Chincoteague (see fig. 1.2). Watermen and fishermen carry on a brisk trade, and the island is famous for its salt oysters and clams, cultivated on leased tideflats, or "rocks," and on public grounds. Crabbing is also popular, especially in the early summertime when the blue crabs come out of their winter hibernation in the Chincoteague Bay mud. The second largest industry is tourism. Each year nearly 1.5 million visitors flock to the beautiful beaches, to the Wildlife Refuge on Assateague, and to the Pony Penning and Carnival. A long causeway connects Chincoteague to the mainland.

Figure 1.2. The tiny island community on Chincoteague welcomes visitors and carries on a thriving seafood industry.

Figure 1.3. Detail of Assateague.

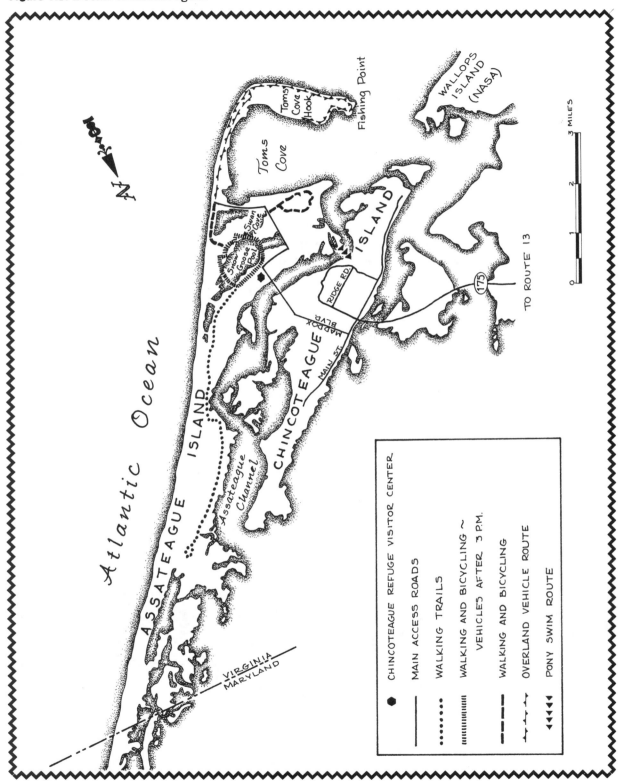

Assateague Island (see fig. 1.3) has been built over centuries from sand raised by waves from the ocean floor. It is ever-changing in shape: even the 2.5-mile-long Tom's Cove Hook did not exist 150 years ago. It has been formed as strong currents pulled into Chincoteague Channel deposit sand along the way. Visitors find white-sand beaches rising from the ocean and merging into dunes covered with American beachgrass. Moving inland they find myrtle brush, then loblolly pine and some hardwood trees.

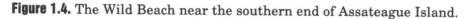

Figure 1.4. The Wild Beach near the southern end of Assateague Island.

Legend has it that early in the sixteenth century a Spanish galleon loaded with Moorish ponies was wrecked off the coast of Assateague. The few ponies that survived struggled ashore (see fig. 1.4) and became the ancestors of the herds that roam the island today (see fig. 1.5).

Figure 1.5. Are there really wild horses on Assateague Island? Indeed there are, and they are so wild that visitors are cautioned to view them only from a distance because they bite and kick.

The Chincoteague National Wildlife Refuge was established in 1943 as a wintering area for waterfowl. During the early 1900s, the populations of waterbirds that wintered on the Delmarva peninsula had been drastically diminished, due in part to hunting and in part to the loss of coastal wetlands to agricultural, industrial, and residential development. Today, more than 300 species of birds have been identified in the refuge, including great egrets, pintailed ducks, and great blue herons. Snow geese, Canada geese, and tundra swans arrive in late autumn (see fig. 1.6).

Figure 1.6. Waterfowl on Swan Cove.

In addition to horses and waterfowl, the refuge is home to whitetail deer (see fig. 1.7), Sika deer, raccoons, red fox, muskrats, and cottontail rabbits. Two endangered species are found in the protected area—the rare Delmarva Peninsula fox squirrel and the piping plover. Nesting areas of the piping plover are closed to all public access from March 15 through August 31.

Figure 1.7. In *Misty of Chincoteague*, Paul first sighted the Phantom and Misty in these woods near Tom's Cove. A careful examination of this picture will reveal a deer in the trees.

There is a 3.5-mile trail for hikers and bicyclists through the refuge on Assateague. It is open to automobiles after 3:00 P.M. Miles of hiking trails lace the island, and cars can travel the main access route to the Tom's Cove area. The Visitor's Center offers tours and interpretive programs.

When Marguerite Henry went to Chincoteague Island to see the Pony Penning Day, she was observing a tradition that began in the 1600s. In those days, unclaimed horses were captured and marked by the colonists and used to renew their supply of workhorses. The ancient roundup day was marked by fellowship and festivity. Later, when the islands were being settled, fire was a constant threat to property and life. A hand-pump fire engine was purchased in 1905, but disastrous fires in 1920 and 1924 convinced the townspeople that better planning was needed, so the Chincoteague Volunteer Fire Company was organized. It was decided that the fire department needed to purchase an American LaFrance pumper with a 750-gallon capacity and 2,000 feet of hose. They needed to raise a lot of money to pay for the equipment.

An ingenious plan was devised based upon the traditional pony roundup begun in the seventeenth century. In July of 1924, the firemen held a carnival for all the people of the island and added a roundup of the ponies on Assateague Island. The ponies were made to swim across the channel to Chincoteague and some were sold at an auction to benefit the Fire Company and buy the much-needed equipment. Every July since then, except for the World War II years of 1942 and 1943, the firemen have held their Carnival and Pony Penning to finance fire protection on the island. The Chincoteague Fire Department (see fig. 1.8) officially owns all the wild ponies on Assateague Island. When the federal government bought the Virginia part of the island in 1943 for a fish and wildlife refuge, special consideration was given to the relationship of the Fire Department and their ponies.

Figure 1.8. The Chincoteague Fire Department.

Though the legend surrounding the origin of the wild ponies of Assateague is colorful, few historians accept it as fact. Most agree that early colonists used the islands to graze their livestock after free-roaming cattle, horses, and goats began damaging crops on the mainland. Laws were being passed requiring fencing and taxing of livestock as a means of limiting crop damage, so the frugal settlers simply moved them to the offshore islands. Those early horses are believed to be the ancestors of today's wild ponies (see fig. 1.9).

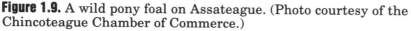

Figure 1.9. A wild pony foal on Assateague. (Photo courtesy of the Chincoteague Chamber of Commerce.)

The ponies on Assateague are split into two herds, one in Virginia and one in Maryland. A fence keeps the two herds separated. To protect the island ecology, the herd populations are carefully limited. The Virginia herd is controlled at between 120 and 150 animals by selling young ponies at the Pony Penning Auction.

The ponies eat the salt marsh grass and American beechgrass that grows abundantly on the island (see fig. 1.10), and they drink fresh water from the natural ponds (see fig. 1.11). As described in *Misty*, the herd has divided into bands of from 2 to 10 horses, and each band is made up of a stallion, his mares, and their foals. The only enemies the ponies have are the mosquitoes and biting flies that are so abundant and ferocious in the summer that the horses are often forced to wade into the surf for relief.

Figure 1.10. A band of wild ponies grazes on the marsh grass. (Photo courtesy of the Chincoteague Chamber of Commerce.)

Figure 1.11. A "gut" in the center of Assateague is one of the freshwater sources for ponies and other island wildlife.

Pony Penning is held the last Wednesday and Thursday in July, and thousands of visitors crowd into Chincoteague for the festivities. On Wednesday morning, the firemen "cowboys" round up the Assateague pony herd, which is driven to swim the quarter-mile channel from the westernmost point of Assateague to the landing spot close to Chincoteague Memorial Park (see fig. 1.12).

Figure 1.12. The ponies swim this quarter-mile stretch of Chincoteague Channel. (Photo courtesy of the Chincoteague Chamber of Commerce.)

Figure 1.13. Bunting Road.

After the ponies have rested, they are driven down Bunting Road (see fig. 1.13) amid cheering crowds toward Main Street and then on to the Carnival Grounds (see fig. 1.14). As described in the Misty series, the Ladies Auxiliary of the Volunteer Fire Department provides lunch for the visitors immediately after the pony swim.

Figure 1.14. This sign stands just outside the Carnival Grounds.

Figure 1.15. The ponies are housed in this shady pen until the festivities begin.

The auction takes place on Thursday. Today, the average bid for a pony is $525, but the highest bid ever was $2,500 in 1989. The ponies are sold as pets to be loved and cared for by their new owners. Those owners must be able to provide safe, comfortable travel arrangements for their ponies.

After the foals and yearlings are auctioned on Thursday, the remaining ponies are driven to swim back to Assateague.

Figure 1.16. In *Sea Star: Orphan of Chincoteague,* Paul and Maureen discover a dead mare and her tiny foal on the shore of Tom's Cove. According to the description in the book, this location in Tom's Cove is where they found Sea Star.

On Ash Wednesday in March 1962 a freak storm hit the islands and caused massive damage. Wallops Island, now a National Aeronautics and Space Administration site, served as an evacuation center for the residents forced to flee Chincoteague. The story of that storm is recounted by Marguerite Henry in *Stormy, Misty's Foal.* As in the book, the Islanders helped one another rebuild the devastated town. The United States Corps of Engineers has since deepened and widened the Gut that runs from one end of Chincoteague to the other so that, hopefully, with better drainage, the type of flooding seen in 1962 will not occur again. The book *Tidal Surge* (Eastern Shore Printers, 1983) contains many photographs of the storm and interviews with residents who survived its fury.

Nearly half the wild ponies on Assateague were drowned in the storm. Contributions from children all over the country poured into the Misty Disaster Fund to help the firemen save the Assateague ponies. The firemen contacted people who had purchased a pony at the auction, and Misty went on tour to raise money for the Disaster Fund. The horses they were able to buy back with money from the fund brought the wild herd's strength back to normal.

The islanders are proud of their famous pony, Misty, and are happy to point out places in town that are significant to her story. Her hoofprints are set in concrete in front of the village movie theater. The Assateague ponies have become a strong influence on the town and are national favorites.

Figure 1.17. This house was the home of Grandpa, Grandma, Paul, and Maureen Beebe. The road that leads to it is known as Beebe Road. Today, a trailer park stands on the land that was once the pony farm.

For More Information

Chincoteague Chamber of Commerce
P.O. Box 258
Chincoteague, VA 23336

Assateague Island National Seashore
Route 611
7206 National Seashore Lane
Berlin, MD 21811

Assateague State Park
Route 611
7307 Stephen Decatur Highway
Berlin, MD 21811

Chincoteague National Wildlife Refuge
P.O. Box 62
Chincoteague, VA 23336

Extended Activities

Map A—Chincoteague Island

1. On map A (page 22), circle the following places:

    A. The Beebe Pony Ranch
    B. The Fire House
    C. The Fire Company Carnival Grounds
    D. The Island Theater where Misty's hoofprint is enshrined in concrete
    E. Pony Swim Landing

Map B—Outline Map of Delmarva Peninsula

2. On map B (page 23), label the following:

    A. The Atlantic Ocean
    B. The Chesapeake Bay
    C. Delaware
    D. Virginia
    E. Maryland
    F. Assateague
    G. Chincoteague

Map C—Eastern United States Railroads

3. *A Pictorial Life Story of Misty* by Marguerite Henry (Macmillan Child Group, 1976) recounts how the real-life Misty, only a few months old, traveled from Chincoteague to Marguerite Henry's home near Chicago. Misty arrived in Geneva, Illinois, aboard the Chicago and Northwestern Railroad and was loaded on a Railway Express truck and shipped to the Henry's home in Wayne, Illinois. Examine map C (page 24), which shows some of the rail lines in the eastern United States, and answer the following questions:

   A. If Misty were to make the same trip today, how far would she travel?
   B. Through what states would she travel?
   C. At what point would she be closest to your home?

Questions and Activities

4. Chincoteague and Assateague are islands, which means they are entirely surrounded by water. They are located just off the coast of a piece of the mainland surrounded on three sides by water. What is the geographic term used for a piece of land with water on three sides?

5. In what state

   A. was Misty born?
   B. was Stormy born?
   C. was Marguerite Henry born?

6. In which of the three Delmarva Peninsula states would you be if you

   A. were in the city of Princess Anne?
   B. searched for animals in the Bombay Hook National Wildlife Refuge?
   C. visited the village of Birdsnest?
   D. waded in the Choptank River?
   E. sailed under the Chesapeake Bay Bridge and into the Atlantic Ocean?
   F. drove on U.S. Route 50?

7. What highway could you take to travel through all three states on the Delmarva Peninsula?

8. Find a map of the Chesapeake Bay region. Following these directions, find and name these places:

   A. A large body of water 70 miles due east of the United States Naval Academy.
   B. A city 45 miles northeast of our nation's capital.
   C. A restored colonial town 50 miles southeast of the capital of Virginia where you can visit with people who are dressed in the styles of George Washington's day.
   D. A presidential estate located near a city 115 miles northeast of Roanoke, Virginia.

9. Your family has asked you for suggestions of places to go on vacation this summer. You want to go to Chincoteague. Develop some convincing points for them to consider about visiting the island. Include:

A. the distance from your home by automobile,
B. the probable number of overnight stops along the way,
C. the time you estimate would be needed for the entire trip,
D. interesting places to see along the route,
E. things to do and see on Chincoteague and Assateague and in the area.

Map A—Chincoteague Island.

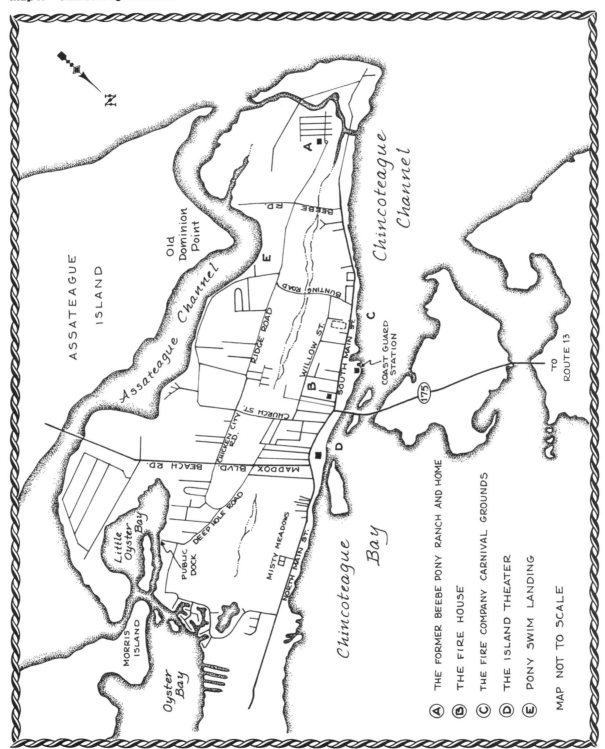

ASSATEAGUE ISLAND

Old Dominion Point

Assateague Channel

Chincoteague Channel

BEEBE RD.

E

BUNTING ROAD

RIDGE ROAD

WILLOW ST.

SOUTH MAIN ST.

C

COAST GUARD STATION

B

175

TO ROUTE 13

CHURCH ST.

CHICKEN CITY RD.

D

MADDOX BLVD.

BEACH RD.

DEEP HOLE ROAD

MISTY MEADOWS

NORTH MAIN ST.

PUBLIC DOCK

Chincoteague Bay

Little Oyster Bay

MORRIS ISLAND

Oyster Bay

(A) THE FORMER BEEBE PONY RANCH AND HOME

(B) THE FIRE HOUSE

(C) THE FIRE COMPANY CARNIVAL GROUNDS

(D) THE ISLAND THEATER

(E) PONY SWIM LANDING

MAP NOT TO SCALE

Map B—Outline Map of Delmarva Peninsula.

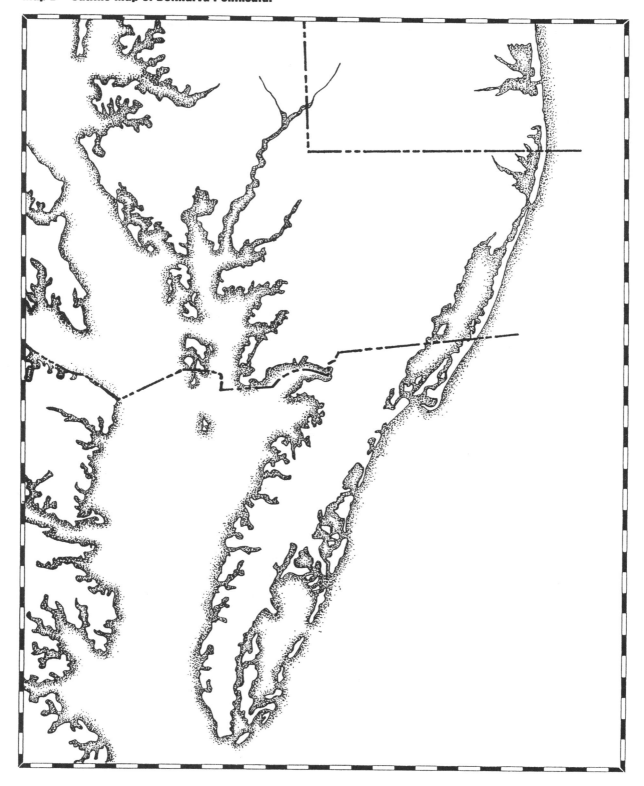

Map C—Eastern United States Railroads.

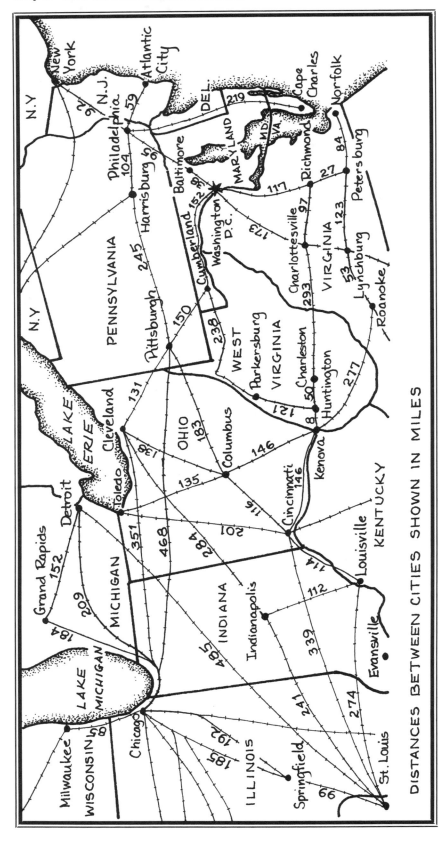

For Further Reading

Other Books by Marguerite Henry

Album of Horses. Chicago: Rand McNally, 1951. 112 pages.
 Twenty breeds of horses are examined in an interesting, informative text that mixes facts and legend and is accompanied by stunning illustrations.

Benjamin West and His Cat Grimalkin. 1947. Reprint. New York: Macmillan, 1987. 147 pages.
 The Quaker childhood of the famous American painter is told in this happy tale that is also a cat story.

Black Gold. Chicago: Rand McNally, 1957. 172 pages.
 The story of a courageous and determined Kentucky Derby winner and his faithful trainer and rider.

Born to Trot. Chicago: Rand McNally, 1950. 219 pages.
 Filled with the history of harness racing, this book is about real people and real events woven into a story about Rosalind, the world champion trotting mare; her young owner, Gibson White; and Hambletonian, the greatest trotter of them all.

Brighty of the Grand Canyon. Chicago: Rand McNally, 1953. 222 pages.
 This story is based on the life of a real burro who traveled the trails of the Grand Canyon in freedom, befriended a prospector, and solved a mystery. Winner of the William Allen White Children's Book Award in 1956.

Cinnabar, the One O'Clock Fox. Chicago: Rand McNally, 1956. 154 pages.
 A fantasy about a fox named Cinnabar, his vixen Vicky, and their four cubs, and about Cinnabar's adventures with hunters and hounds.

Dear Readers and Riders. Chicago: Rand McNally, 1969. 223 pages.
 Each chapter in this book answers questions from readers about a different Henry story. Three chapters are devoted to the Misty series, and the truth behind the fiction is revealed.

Gaudenzia, Pride of the Palio. Chicago: Rand McNally, 1960. 237 pages.
 The drama and danger of the Palio races in Siena, Italy, are seen through this story of a real horse and the boy who trained and rode her.

The Illustrated Marguerite Henry. Chicago: Rand McNally, 1980. 128 pages.
 Readers are introduced to the illustrators who have worked with Henry over the years. She tells how each of her books took shape visually and describes the collaboration between author and illustrator.

Justin Morgan Had a Horse. Chicago: Rand McNally, 1954. 164 pages.
This story of the brave little workhorse who became the sire of the Morgan breed of horses is built around the true history of founder of the line. This book is a Junior Literary Guild selection, winner of the Junior Scholastic Gold Seal Award and the Award of the Friends of Literature in 1946. A Newbery Honor Book, 1947.

King of the Wind. 1948. Reprint. New York: Macmillan, 1988. 172 pages.
Sham, the great Godolphin Arabian, ancestor of Man o' War and other great thoroughbreds, had a loyal friend who stayed by his side through incredible hardship. This is the story of a great horse and the boy who loved him. Winner of the Newbery Award, 1948.

Mustang, Wild Spirit of the West. Chicago: Rand McNally, 1966. 222 pages.
Annie Johnson was a determined woman who led the fight to save the wild mustangs from hunters who preyed on them from airplanes and trucks.

A Pictorial Life Story of Misty. Chicago: Rand McNally, 1976. 144 pages.
Want to see how the real characters actually looked, what they said, and how they acted? The real Misty and the Beebe family members are introduced in warm, affectionate terms and in hundreds of photographs. This book is the perfect companion to a reading of the Misty series.

Robert Fulton, Boy Craftsman. Indianapolis, IN: Bobbs-Merrill, 1945. 187 pages.
Known primarily as the inventor of the steamboat, Robert Fulton had a variety of other interests and talents, many of which are revealed in this interesting biography.

San Domingo: The Medicine Hat Stallion. Chicago: Rand McNally, 1972. 230 pages.
Set in the Nebraska Territory in the mid-1800s, this novel tells the story of Peter Lundy, who overcomes a difficult childhood and the loss of his beloved Indian pony to grow to manhood as a rider for the Pony Express.

Wagging Tails: An Album of Dogs. Chicago: Rand McNally, 1955. 64 pages.
Twenty-five purebred dogs and one mongrel are described in appearance, history, and personality.

White Stallion of Lipizza. 1964. Reprint. Chicago: Rand McNally, 1985. 116 pages.
The ancient art of classical riding is described in this story of the Spanish Court Riding School in Vienna and one of its students.

The Assateague Ponies

Bullaty, Sonja, and Angelo Lomeo. *The Little Wild Ponies.* New York: Simon & Schuster, 1987. 24 pages.
A photographic essay about the lives of the ponies of Assateague Island.

Ford, Barbara, and Ronald R. Keiper. *The Island Ponies: An Environmental Study of Their Life on Assateague.* New York: Morrow, 1979.
The scientific study of the role of the island ponies in the ecology of the barrier island is described. The book is illustrated with many black-and-white photos.

Grosvenor, Donna K. *The Wild Ponies of Assateague Island.* Washington, DC: National Geographic Society, 1975. 30 pages.
In simple text and vivid photographs, the life of the island ponies is described. Pony Penning is discussed and portrayed in action-filled pictures.

Rood, Ronald. *Hundred Acre Welcome: The Story of a Chincoteague Pony.* Brattleboro, VT: Stephen Greene Press, 1967. 132 pages.
The author and his family visited Chincoteague during Pony Penning and "impulse-bought" a little colt. As they tried to return to their Vermont home with their purchase, they realized the problems their new pet would bring. Here is a factual account of the pony's fate as seen through the eyes of a naturalist.

Scott, Jack. *Island of Wild Horses.* New York: Putnam, 1978. 61 pages.
A well-organized, beautifully illustrated book packed with information describing the history, physical characteristics, life, habitat, and management problems of the Chincoteague ponies.

Ponies and Miniature Horses

LaBonte, Gail I. *The Miniature Horse.* Minneapolis, MN: Dillon, 1990. 59 pages.
Miniature horses in America are described, and information on their rearing and use is given. Sources for more information are included with a glossary and index.

Lavine, Sigmund, and Brigid Casey. *Wonders of Ponies.* New York: Dodd, Mead, 1980. 80 pages.
The uses and characteristics of ancient and present-day ponies are discussed. Some famous ponies are introduced, and there is an interesting discussion of the cross-breeding that produced the unique conformation of the Chincoteague pony.

Patent, Dorothy Hinshaw. *Miniature Horses.* New York: Dutton Children's Books, 1991. 48 pages.
Miniature horses are like their larger family members, just much smaller. The two types of miniatures are described in text and color photos.

———. *A Picture Book of Ponies.* New York: Holiday House, 1983.
The various breeds of ponies are described in photographs and in text.

Rodenas, Paula. *The Random House Book of Horses and Horsemanship.* New York: Random House, 1991. 180 pages.
A broad scope of information is provided, illustrated with photographs, drawings, and diagrams.

2

Wethersfield, Connecticut

The Setting for Elizabeth George Speare's

The Witch of Blackbird Pond
Houghton Mifflin, 1958. 249 pages.

Book Summary

It is in the spring of 1687 when Kit Tyler sails up the Connecticut River aboard the brigantine *Dolphin* to find her new home in Wethersfield. Orphaned, penniless, and alone since the death of her beloved grandfather a few months before, Kit had been forced to give up her luxurious lifestyle and sell her family's large plantation in Barbados to pay debts. She even had to sell her personal slave to buy her passage to Connecticut. With seven small trunks filled with the last of her elegant and colorful clothes, Kit has come in search of her only relative, an aunt whom she has never seen.

Wethersfield is a dreary little Puritan settlement, and Kit is dismayed by the cool welcome she receives from her aunt's husband, Mathew Wood. He is a somber, uncompromising, and hardworking man who is shocked by Kit's finery and gay, impulsive manner. Kit is readily accepted by her kind aunt, however, and by her cousins, beautiful Judith and the lovely but lame Mercy. Kit works hard to fit into the harsh, puritanical life of her new family, but, despite her best efforts, her unconventional behavior continually scandalizes them and raises the suspicions of the dour townsfolk.

Even Kit's politics run counter to those of the family. She has been raised as a Royalist by her grandfather, but her uncle and many of the townspeople are turning against the Crown as they struggle to retain their independence and Colonial charter. William Ashby, the son of a well-to-do landholder, begins courting Kit, but she finds his company boring. Nor is she interested in the handsome young divinity student, John Holbrook, whom her cousin Judith finds so attractive.

Kit befriends Hannah Tupper, an old Quaker woman suspected of witchcraft, and continues the friendship in secret when her uncle has forbidden it. When an epidemic sweeps through the community, killing several children, some of the townspeople conclude that Hannah Tupper is the cause of the problem.

Having recovered from the illness herself, Kit tirelessly nurses Judith and the dangerously ill Mercy. When she learns of plans to arrest Hannah, Kit runs to her aid and helps her escape from the rioting mob. Nat Eaton, the young sailor who originally brought Kit to Wethersfield aboard his father's ship, the *Dolphin*, comes to Kit's aid and provides a safe haven for the old woman. The next day, Kit is arrested herself on charges of witchcraft and is imprisoned in the constable's shed. Alone and frightened, she waits in vain for William Ashby to come to her rescue.

Nat Eaton makes a surprise appearance at Kit's trial and brings along the young daughter of her main accuser. The girl is able to provide evidence of Kit's innocence, and Kit is released to her fair-minded family and is accepted by the townspeople. Now William returns to court her, but Kit ends their relationship. It is Nat Eaton to whom she turns and they make plans to marry the next spring. Kit and Nat happily plan her future as the wife of a ship captain who makes regular winter voyages to Barbados, but returns to New England each summer.

About the Author

Elizabeth George Speare was born in Melrose, Massachusetts, a suburb of Boston, in 1908. In *More Junior Authors* and *More Books by More People*, Elizabeth says her childhood was a happy one with family reunions, picnics, and summers spent in a town south of Boston with a wonderful view of the ocean.[1] During those summers she discovered that she loved to write; through her childhood and high school she wrote constantly.

Elizabeth went to Smith College for her freshman year but graduated from Boston University in 1930 with a B.A. in English. She received her master's in English in 1932 and then taught high school English for four years in Rockland and Auburn, Massachusetts.

She married Alden Speare in 1936 and moved to Wethersfield, Connecticut. Their son, Alden Jr., was born in 1939, and a daughter, Mary Elizabeth, was born in 1942. She spent the next 10 years raising her children and publishing practical magazine articles for homemakers and a few one-act plays.

While reading a book on the history of the Connecticut River, Elizabeth read an account of the capture of Susanna Johnson and her family. She researched material for a book based on the true-life adventure. *Calico Captive,* published in 1957 was selected as an ALA Notable Children's Book in 1958. This success encouraged Speare to continue writing, but for some time she struggled to find a suitable subject. As she studied the history of Wethersfield, intriguing characters began to form.[2] Her task became that of finding a suitable story.

She then read an account of a young girl who came to Boston from Barbados. The girl had written to her parents in the Caribbean complaining of the harshness of her restrictive life in Boston. Speare wondered what would have been the case if the girl had come to dour, Puritan Wethersfield instead of the comfort and culture of Boston, and so *The Witch of Blackbird Pond* was born. The book, published in 1958, won the 1959 Newbery Medal.

The restoration and opening of Old Sturbridge Village in Sturbridge, Massachusetts, was the inspiration for a series of informational booklets on period life and times in the town. One of these was Speare's *Child Life in New England, 1790-1840*, published by Old Sturbridge Village and sold there.

The Bronze Bow (1961), which she thought could be read in Sunday schools, was set in the Palestine during the Roman occupation and dealt with the life of Christ. To her surprise it became a popular favorite and won the 1962 Newbery Award. In 1961, the Speares left Wethersfield and moved to Easton, Connecticut.

Another nonfiction book, *Life in Colonial America,* followed in 1963. In 1967, she wrote her only adult book, *The Prospering,* a tale based on events and people in the mid-eighteenth century New England. A very different Wethersfield appears briefly as a setting in this novel. The 50 years that have elapsed have brought wealth, prosperity, and charm to the village.

It wasn't until 1983 that Speare published another book. *The Sign of the Beaver* is the story of a boy who, in the year 1768, is left alone in the family cabin in Maine while his father returns to Massachusetts. Designated a Newbery Honor Book in 1984, it received the first Scott O'Dell Award for Historical Fiction.

In 1989, Elizabeth George Speare was the recipient of the Laura Ingalls Wilder Award for "a substantial and lasting contribution to children's literature."

Setting:
Wethersfield, Connecticut

Old Wethersfield, from Its Beginnings to 1687

Figure 2.1.

Wethersfield is centrally located in Connecticut, only four miles south of Hartford, just off Interstate 91. The Connecticut River, the longest in New England, lies just to the east, and the valley is the watershed for tributaries in northern New Hampshire and a large area to the south, including the White and Green Mountains and the Berkshire Hills. Annual spring flooding of the riverside meadows contributes to the fertility of the soil, and streams and broad swamplands are prevalent.

The Wethersfield area was originally settled by Native Americans of the Wongunk tribe who called the place "Pyquang," which means "cleared land." They hunted the many animals that lived in the forests, such as bear, fox, wolves, wildcats, deer, beaver, squirrels, and raccoons, and they caught the fish and hunted the waterfowl that were plentiful in the streams and the river. The women and children raised corn, beans, and squash in the fertile riverside meadows.

Since the mid-sixteenth century, the Wongunk group had been oppressed by the Pequot tribe who lived in what is now the southeastern part of Connecticut. When the English settled in the Massachusetts Colony, the Wongunk thought their guns might afford protection from the Pequot. So in 1633 they sent a delegation of two tribal chieftains and a Native American who had traveled to England and could speak English to the settlement in Charlestown. There they asked the settlers to move their homes to the banks of the "Great River of Sweet Water," where fine homesites were located close to fertile fields and abundant hunting grounds. Though the Puritans turned down their offer, one of the company, a trader named John Oldham, was interested and traveled to the area to explore the possibilities. He realized the advantages of the location and returned to Watertown, Massachusetts, to encourage other men anxious to make a change to join him in the move.

In the fall of 1634, Oldham returned to Pyquaug with nine others. The group later became known as the "Ten Adventurers." They spent the winter in huts on the riverbank, and the next year brought their families and friends to form "a new Church government on the River Connecticut." They built huts, planted crops, and began a settlement in earnest. The land was purchased from the Wongunks in 1636, and the town was officially founded. Tradition has it that the town was named in honor of the wife of one of the Adventurers, Leonard Chester. His wife, Mary, was supposed to have been descended from the lords of Wethersfield in England. There is no confirmation of this story.

Wethersfield was founded by English from Massachusetts Bay and Plymouth who were, for the most part, sincere Puritans. The members of this religious sect had adopted the ideas of the Protestant Revolution and wanted to "purify" the established church in England. Many left England and came to America because of their religious beliefs and for economic reasons.

Only men who were church members and landowners were allowed to vote. They adhered strictly to Puritan belief and had very little tolerance for those who did not share those beliefs. Their hostility toward the Quakers is authentically represented in *The Witch of Blackbird Pond.*

There was no separation of church and state; the church was the government. The founding of the First Church of Christ in Wethersfield took place in 1636 and heralded the founding of the town. Kit Tyler was at the mercy of this Puritan church government when she came to trial in *The Witch of Blackbird Pond.*

Figure 2.2. The Meeting House.

The Meeting House shown in figure 2.2 was constructed during the years 1761-1764 and is the third meeting house erected in Wethersfield. The spire was patterned after the Old South Church in Boston, one of the most beautiful examples of Colonial architecture in New England. The bricks for the church were made locally, and the mortar was made of clam shells brought upriver from Long Island Sound. Many members of the congregation found it hard to contribute financially when the Meeting House was built, so ropes of onions were accepted instead of taxes. The onions were sold to finance the church, and that is how it came to be known as "the church that onions built."[3] The flagpole to the right in figure 2.2 marks the site of the first Meeting House.

Figure 2.3. This monument marks the site of Wethersfield's first Meeting House.

At the base of the flagpole is a monument that marks the site of the first Meeting House, built during the years 1645-1647. The stocks and pillory must have also occupied this prominent spot in the center of Meeting House Square. According to John Willard, the first Meeting House was a small, rough structure made of squared-off logs covered with hand-sawn boards. The boards were covered with clay and were called "clay-boards," which is where the term *clap-boards* comes from.[4] The Meeting House of *The Witch of Blackbird Pond* was the second church and was only two years old when Kit Tyler arrived in 1687. Measuring 50 feet square, with doors and windows, it was larger than the first meeting house.

Figure 2.4. This view looks across Main Street from River Road to the location of the fictional Wood home. In Kit's day, Hamner Park (in the foreground) was the site of a small pond.

The original plan of the village of Wethersfield was patterned after an English village. Homes were set on small plots of land of two or three acres. In addition, villagers would own shares of property in the woodlands, the meadows, and pastures where farming operations were carried out by hand or with the occasional use of oxen (see figs. 2.5 and 2.7). When Matthew Wood went off to work in the south meadow, he was following the practice of the time. The fields were often distant from a farmer's home.

The restored home near the Commons seen in figure 2.6 was built in 1637 for George Hubbard. It was originally one room with another room above. In the late 1600s, there was a silver and textile shop in the house, and it would have been one of the small cabins Kit passed on her first muddy trip from the harbor through the dreary settlement to her uncle's house.

In April of 1637, the old enemies of the Wongunks, the Pequot, attacked the settlement, killing nine people as they worked in the fields. Twenty cows were slain and two young girls were captured but were later returned, unharmed. A militia was raised of men from Hartford, Windsor, and Wethersfield, and the Pequots were routed at Mystic, Connecticut. The militia was maintained by the Colony for many years, and it was this group that John Holbrook joined to put down an Indian uprising in some towns north of Hadley, Massachusetts, in 1687 in *The Witch of Blackbird Pond.*

Figure 2.5. Part of the original Commons (pasture land for the town livestock) remains in this area near the Wethersfield Cove

Figure 2.6. A restored house built in 1637.

Figure 2.7. Based upon a map developed by Fran Stremlau and provided courtesy of the Wethersfield Public Library.

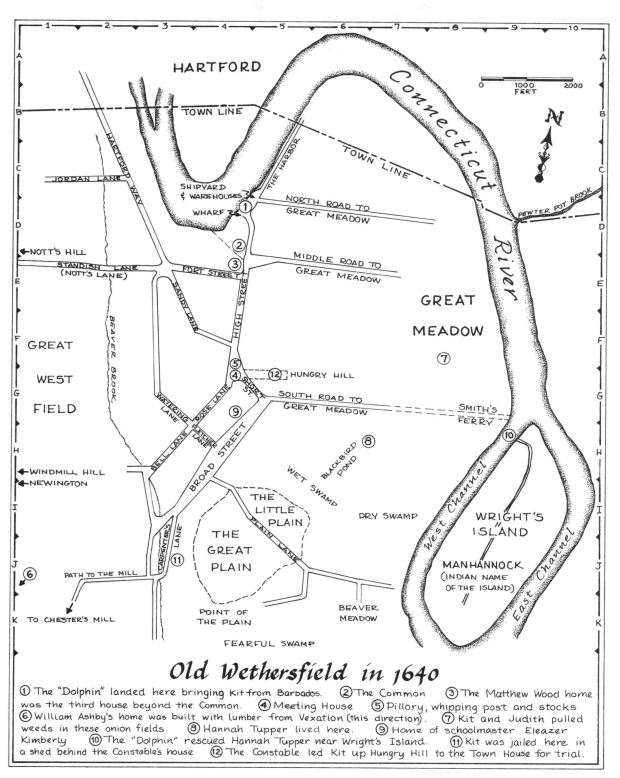

Old Wethersfield in 1640

① The "Dolphin" landed here bringing Kit from Barbados. ② The Common ③ The Matthew Wood home was the third house beyond the Common. ④ Meeting House ⑤ Pillory, whipping post and stocks ⑥ William Ashby's home was built with lumber from Vexation (this direction). ⑦ Kit and Judith pulled weeds in these onion fields. ⑧ Hannah Tupper lived here. ⑨ Home of schoolmaster Eleazer Kimberly ⑩ The "Dolphin" rescued Hannah Tupper near Wright's Island. ⑪ Kit was jailed here in a shed behind the Constable's house ⑫ The Constable led Kit up Hungry Hill to the Town House for trial.

The cooperation of the three towns continued, and in 1639, they adopted what is thought to be the first written constitution in America. It was called the Fundamental Orders, which were rules and regulations drawn up to ensure the welfare and safety of the settlers. When the Connecticut Charter was finally granted in 1662, the provisions of the Fundamental Orders were included in it. The dispute over the Connecticut Charter is vividly described in *The Witch of Blackbird Pond* when Matthew Wood so ardently opposes Governor Andros's intention to set aside the charter and annex Connecticut to Massachusetts in 1687.

When William Ashby tells Matthew that the charter is safely hidden away, he is referring to an actual incident in Connecticut history. On October 31, 1687, Governor Andros demanded the charter from Governor Treat just as recounted by Speare. During a meeting that evening between Andros and Connecticut leaders, the charter disappeared. Although Andros now had the government of the colony in his hands, he did not acquire the charter, which, legend has it, was hidden in a large oak tree in Hartford thereafter known as "The Charter Oak."

The affairs of local government were handled by town meeting, a gathering of all the citizens who were eligible to vote. The town meetings elected Selectmen who handled the town expenses, cared for the poor, built and repaired bridges, paid all church expenses, paid bounties on wolves and blackbirds, and hired the herders who cared for the livestock grazing on the Commons. Matthew Wood was a Selectman and sat with them at Kit's trial, which was held in the Meeting House.

The chief law enforcement officer of the town was the constable, an unpopular job. Many citizens preferred to pay a fine of 40 shillings rather than serve as constable, so when the constable's wife complained to Kit that she and her husband didn't like the work and would be glad when his term was up, she was reflecting the popular opinion of the day.

There was no jail in Wethersfield, so Kit was held in a shed at the back of the constable's house on Carpenter Lane. In addition to carrying out the orders of the Court, the constable was the tax collector and was in charge of the watch and the militia.

Colonial law in 1678 required that each town 30 or more families appoint some person to teach reading and writing. Wethersfield, however, had hired a schoolmaster as early as 1650, when a Mr. William Janes of New Haven was employed to teach the children. The schoolmaster of *The Witch of Blackbird Pond*, Eleazur Kimberley, was first appointed in 1661, and was later to serve as the Secretary of the Connecticut Colony. Other schoolmasters were employed from 1665 to 1677, but in that year, the distinguished Mr. Kimberley was again put in charge of the education of Wethersfield youngsters, a position he was to hold for almost 25 years.

Like many women in Colonial New England, Mercy and Kit ran a "dame school," a private school rather like a kindergarten, where 8 or 10 little boys and girls learned to read and to do simple arithmetic. This kitchen school would be the only formal education many girls would ever receive.

Corn and other vegetables were grown in the fertile fields that surrounded the town, but the area became famous for the Wethersfield Red Onion, which seems to have been grown at a very early date (see fig. 2.8). Barrels of onions were shipped to New York City and other coastal cities and to Europe and the West Indies. Up to 1,500,000 barrels of onions were shipped annually, and when Kit and Judith weeded the onion fields, they were probably performing a common chore in those days.

Figure 2.8. In Kit Tyler's day, onions filled this field near the Connecticut River.

Another popular crop of the times was flax, which was processed and spun into fine thread, then woven into cloth. This was the only readily available thin fabric, for cotton and silk were too expensive for everyday use. The quality of the thread was determined by the spinning wheel operator's skill. Hannah Tupper was able to eke out a living because her reputation as an expert spinner brought customers from the town with flax to be spun.

Besides farming, the oldest industry in Wethersfield was shipbuilding. The first ship constructed there was the *Tryall,* built in 1642. In 1648, a carpenter named Thomas Deming was granted land "by the Landing Place" in the Cove to construct a workyard that was probably the first shipyard in the Connecticut Colony. Soon, ships built, owned, and manned by local men sailed along the coast and to the West Indies with goods produced by the rich valley soil.

In those days, large ships could not navigate the river north of Wethersfield, so all their cargo had to be transferred to flatboats or rafts. The Commons at the Landing became the commercial center of the town, and warehouses were constructed there from 1662 to 1691. Those warehouses were the first things Kit Tyler saw when she disembarked from the *Dolphin.*

Figure 2.9. The Wethersfield Cove and the Old Warehouse.

This warehouse pictured in figure 2.9 is the only one that remains of the six or seven that were built between 1662 and 1691 along the shores of the Connecticut River. At that time, the cove was a bend in the river, but around 1700 the river changed its course and swept away all but this warehouse. A new channel was cut across the meadows and The Cove, though still connected to the river by a narrow cut, was no longer a busy shipping port.

Trade with the West Indies began in 1648 and sugar was brought from there as early as 1662. A report to the Privy Council in 1680 states that among the principal exports from Wethersfield were horses, like those carried on the *Dolphin* that had left the strong stench that bothered Kit on her journey in 1687. Many products were shipped directly to Boston; some were shipped to Barbados and other Caribbean ports where they were traded for sugar, cotton, salt, and rum.

A very real part of Connecticut history was being described when the fictitious Kit Tyler was accused of witchcraft. Between 1647 and 1697, 11 so-called witches were hung in the Colony. This frenzy of witch-hunting preceded the famous Salem witchcraft trials by almost 50 years. Most witches were sent to Hartford for trial and, if convicted, were publicly hanged in the middle of the city.

On December 7, 1648, Wethersfield resident Mary Johnson was convicted of familiarity with the Devil and sentenced to be executed. She had been publicly whipped in Wethersfield two years before and she was found guilty in Hartford primarily because she readily confessed to consorting with the Devil.

John Carrington, a carpenter, and his wife Joanne had come to Wethersfield in 1643 and had a home on Sandy Lane near the corner of Fort Street. On February 20, 1650, they were both convicted of witchcraft and sentenced to death.

Kit Tyler was told about Mary Johnson and she also learned about Katherine Harrison. Katherine was the widow of the well-respected John Harrison who had died in 1666, leaving her with three young daughters. In 1668, Katherine was arrested on a charge of witchcraft and taken to Hartford for trial. She was charged with bringing illness to some people and death to others, with influencing animals to disobey their masters, and with changing her own form. She was found innocent of the charges and freed.

The suspicions of Katherine's neighbors continued, however, and in May of 1669 she was again arrested on similar charges. A jury failed to agree on a guilty verdict, so Katherine was kept in jail until court convened in the fall. This time, she was found guilty, but the Court was not satisfied and sought expert testimony from certain ministers reputed to be experts on the workings of the Devil. She remained in jail until May 1670 when she was ordered to pay her court costs and was then released on the condition that she would leave Wethersfield immediately. The heroic Katherine was undaunted and sued her accusers for slander. Although it is unclear if her suit was successful, two years later Katherine was awarded five pounds for work she had done for her jailer.[5]

Elizabeth George Speare carefully researched the Connecticut witch hunts before she included those episodes in her book. In the basement of the State Library in Hartford, she found ancient ledgers with handwritten records of testimony given at the witchcraft trials. She was shocked at the ridiculous accusations leveled by ignorant and spiteful neighbors against innocent people. The "witches," she found, were often harmless old women who may have been simply independent, or crotchety, or whose behavior differed from the strict, puritanical standards of the majority of the townspeople. That such unfounded tales were believed by basically good people was astonishing to Speare. Some of the testimony she found was included verbatim in the trial of Kit in *The Witch of Blackbird Pond.*

Figure 2.10. The constable and two members of the watch conducted Kit to the Meeting House for her trial. Their route took them up Hungry Hill in the Ancient Burying Ground.

About a mile south of the Cove, the Connecticut river separates, forming a large island. In Kit Tyler's day, this island of about 200 acres was called "Mannhannock" by the Wongunks and "Wright's Island" by the villagers. Up to a dozen men owned property there. It had a navigable channel on each side and it was the island that provided the haven for the *Dolphin* when Kit and Nat led Hannah Tupper there to escape the witch-hunting mob that pursued her.

Though most of the characters in *The Witch of Blackbird Pond* are fictional, some are actual historical figures. In addition to the schoolmaster Eleazur Kimberley, the Reverend John Woodbridge, who visited Mercy's school and sat with those who questioned Kit at her trial, was a real person. He came to Wethersfield as a minister in 1670 and lived there until his death in 1701. He was given a 200-acre farm at the north end of Newington by the town in 1685 to supplement his annual salary of 100 pounds, the use of the parsonage, and 80 loads of wood.

Captain Samuel Talcott, who presided at Kit's trial and escorted Governor Andros from Wethersfield to Hartford, was also a historical figure. According to *The History of Ancient Wethersfield,* by Sherman W. Adams, he was "one of the most influential men in the Col.[ony] and as Capt. of Militia, often in active service; as also in civic offices of Town and Colonial trust."[6] Evidence of the high regard the townspeople held for Sam Talcott is shown by his appointment to the committee charged with the repair and enlargement of the Meeting House in 1674 and later to the committee to make the arrangements for the building of a new Meeting House.

The most prestigious person to appear as a character in *The Witch of Blackbird Pond* is Dr. Gershom Bulkeley, minister, physician, scholar, and outspoken Royalist. Gershom Bulkeley came to Wethersfield in 1667 from New London. He had been negotiating with the town since 1664 to serve as an Officer of the Church and finally arrived at an agreement: an annual salary of 70 pounds, a house, the use of the common lands, transportation of his household goods, and a paid assistant. During the next few years, the townsfolk continued to increase his salary and his land holdings in turn for his continued service in their church. John Willard describes Dr. Bulkeley as being proficient in Latin, Greek, and Dutch, and as an expert surveyor.[7] He had studied medicine and was a much respected Magistrate. In 1676, two years before Kit Tyler arrived in Wethersfield, Bulkeley retired from the ministry because he had developed "a week [*sic*] voice"; from that time he served the village as a physician.

During Sir Edmund Andros's attempt to interfere with the government of Connecticut, Bulkeley went against the political opinions of many of the townspeople with his ardently Royalist stand. His stance gained him the favorable attention of Andros, who appointed Bulkeley to the position of Justice of the Peace. In 1692, Bulkeley and Major Edward Palmes published a tract entitled "Will and Doom, or the Miseries of Connecticut by and under an Usurped and Arbitrary Power, Some Objections against the present prtended Govermt in Connecticut, in New England, In America, Humbly tendered to Concideration"[*sic*]. In it, Bulkeley professes his attachment to the government under Andros and his contempt for the government established under the Colonial Charter. This opinionated paper was sent to England and was useful to those seeking to overthrow all American Colonial Charters.

Figure 2.11. Somewhere in this field known as the Great Meadow was the real Blackbird Pond.

Wethersfield Today

The people of Wethersfield are proud of their historic town, one of the oldest communities in Connecticut. The historic "Old Wethersfield," is listed on the National Register of Historic Places. It was established in 1962 and is the state's largest historic district. Over 116 structures built prior to 1840 still stand, including the home of Silas Deane, who, in 1776, was America's first diplomat; and the Joseph Webb House, where George Washington consulted with General Rochambeau on a strategy that led to the British surrender at Yorktown.

The Buttolph-Williams house was built around 1720 and restored to its original condition in 1947. According to an interview videotaped in this house (*A Visit with Elizabeth George Speare.* 5-96426), it was this building that Elizabeth Speare thought of when she first imagined the Wood home in *The Witch of Blackbird Pond.*[8] Later, she decided it would have been far too grand for the Wood family, but would have been exactly the kind of house William Ashby would build on Broad Street for his bride. The Buttolph-Williams house stands on Broad Street as did the home of Eleazur Kimberley.

Figure 2.12. Wethersfield historic district today.

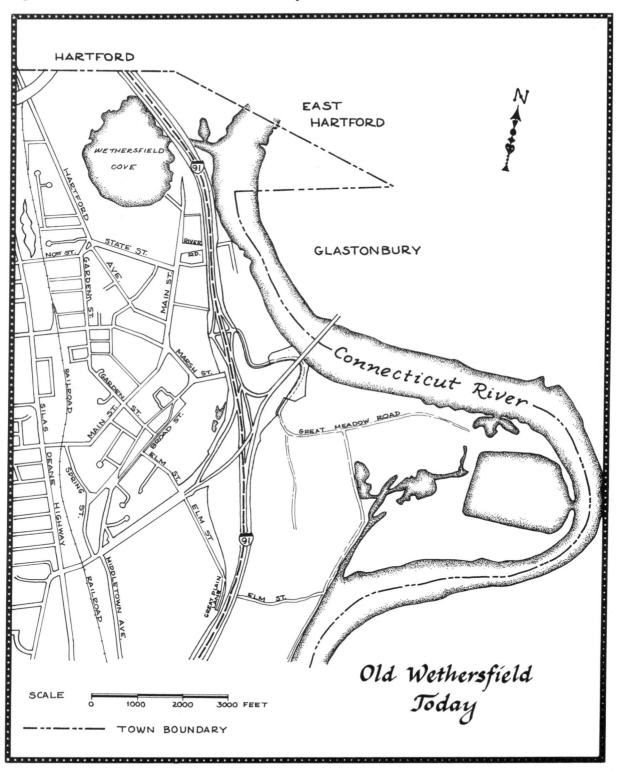

Figure 2.13. The Buttolph-Williams house.

Today, Wethersfield encompasses 13.5 square miles and has a population of about 25,400. It is primarily a suburban community where people come to live and raise their families, but work in larger, nearby communities. Tourism is the largest industry in the town, with thousands of visitors coming every year to visit the historic sites that are open to the public. Wethersfield also has a modest industrial base consisting of tool and die manufacturers, marine terminals for gasoline and fuel oils, frozen food processors, and research and development firms. The Connecticut Light and Power Company's Computer Center and the Northeast Utilities Service Headquarters are located there.

There are 10 churches representing a wide range of religious diversity in Wethersfield as opposed to the one allowed during colonial times. Almost 3,000 students attend the five elementary schools, the Silas Deane Middle School, and the Wethersfield High School. The Wethersfield Public Library offers a full range of programs and services including many materials pertaining to the history of Wethersfield. The children's department of the library has some documents relating to *The Witch of Blackbird Pond.*

Public transportation is provided by the Connecticut Transit bus lines, Amtrak rail service from Hartford, and air service from the Bradley International Airport north of Hartford. There are five major shopping centers in Wethersfield and many antique stores, boutiques, and speciality shops in the historic district. There are a large number of recreational facilities available, including 18 tennis courts, 10 playgrounds, 6 softball fields, 16 soccer fields, 3 swimming pools, and several parks that offer picnicking, boating, fishing, nature trails, and bathing beaches.

Wethersfield is most well known, however, for preservation and presentation of its past. In addition to the Meeting House, the Buttolph-Williams House, and the Ancient Burying Ground, there are a number of interesting museums and old homes open to the public. Chief among these is the Webb-Deane-Stevens Museum, which is made up of three eighteenth-century houses authentically restored on their original sites and furnished to depict colonial homes. The Keeney Memorial Cultural Center, originally a school built in 1893, features a permanent exhibit on local history as well as art shows and a museum store. The Old Academy was originally a school built in 1804. Today, it is the headquarters for the Wethersfield Historical Society and contains a genealogical and research library. There are walking tours of the city offered by the Society and they often arrange special events such as craft fairs, lantern-light tours, and Victorian Christmas celebrations.

For More Information

The Wethersfield Chamber of Commerce
250 Constitution Plaza
Hartford, CT 06103

Wethersfield Historical Society
150 Main Street
Wethersfield, CT 06109

Wethersfield Public Library
515 Silas Deane Highway
Wethersfield, CT 06109

Notes

1. Muriel Fuller, ed., *More Junior Authors* (New York: H. W. Wilson, 1963), 189; Lee Bennett Hopkins, *More Books by More People* (New York: Citation Press, 1974), 330.

2. *A Visit with Elizabeth George Speare,* videotaped interview, Author and Artist Series 5-96426 (Boston: Houghton Mifflin, 1986).

3. Lois M. Weider, *The Wethersfield Story* (Stonington, CT: Pequot Press, 1966), 29.

4. John Willard, *Willard's Wethersfield* (West Hartford, CT: West Hartford Publications, 1975), 30.

5. Willard, *Willard's Wethersfield,* 36.

6. Sherman W. Adams, *The History of Ancient Wethersfield, Vol. I—History* (New York: Grafton Press, 1904), 305.

7. Willard, *Willard's Wethersfield,* 29.

8. *A Visit with Elizabeth George Speare.*

Extended Activities

1. Find an atlas in your school or public library that has a map of the Caribbean Sea. Locate Barbados by using the index in the back of the atlas, then answer the following:

   A. If the *Dolphin* had traveled in an almost straight line, approximately how far was the journey from Barbados to Wethersfield?

   B. Barbados is a part of what island chain?

2. First examine the maps of Old Wethersfield (see fig. 2.7) and Wethersfield today (see fig. 2.12) and make a list of all the changes that have occurred in the last 300 years. Next, divide your list into these two classifications:

   A. Those changes that are as a result of natural causes.

   B. Those changes that are the result of human action.

3. A. In addition to the changes Kit experienced in climate, politics, and religious beliefs, would she also have experienced a change in the time of day when she moved from Barbados to Wethersfield? Find a time zone map in an atlas. Are Wethersfield and Barbados in the same time zone? If not, what is the difference in time?

   B. Suppose you want to call the Wethersfield Historical Association for more information about the town. Their office opens at 10:00 A.M. local time. What time will that be where you are?

   C. Your class is online with a computer network linking your school to a school in Barbados. You have scheduled your next meeting with them for tomorrow at 2:30 P.M. Barbados time. At what local time in your town should your class be ready to communicate with them?

4. Prepare a key for the map of old Wethersfield (see fig. 2.7). Give the map coordinates for the following:

   A. Meeting House
   B. Wharf
   C. Blackbird Pond
   D. The Wood home
   E. Eleazur Kimberly home
   F. Onion fields
   G. Constable's home
   H. The Common

5. Using the descriptions given in the story and the locations on the map of old Wethersfield (fig. 2.7), mark Kit's routes

   A. from the dock where she landed to her uncle's home.
   B. from the Wood house to Hannah's cottage.
   C. from the Constable's shed to the Meeting House.

6. Find the latitude and longitude of Wethersfield, Connecticut, and Barbados. *The Britannica Atlas* (Chicago: Encyclopaedia Britannica, 1979) or *Rand McNally Goode's World Atlas* (Chicago: Rand McNally, 1990) are sources that give the latitude and longitude for most cities and towns in the world. Check the indexes of other atlases in your school or public library. Many have that information.

7. The climograph on page 49 shows the annual temperature and precipitation for one of the locations in the story. The line graph shows the average monthly temperatures, and the bar graph shows the average monthly precipitation. The chart below the graph gives the same data.

Climograph Number 1.

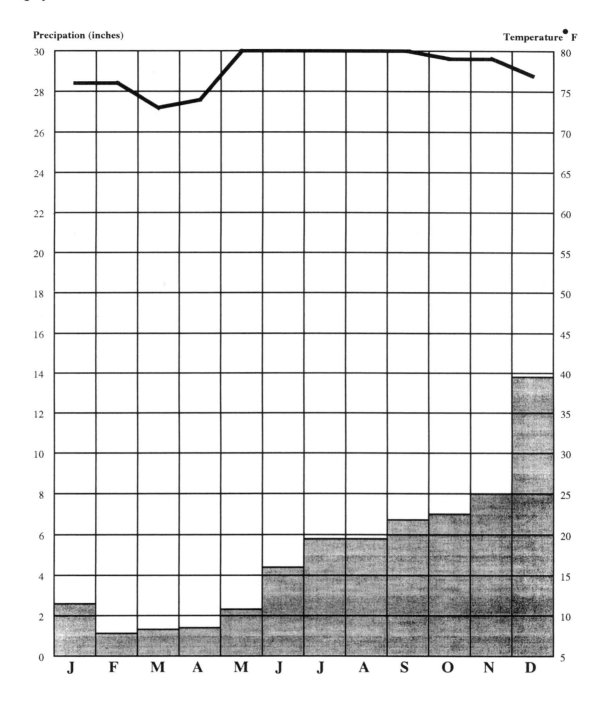

Precipation (inches)   Temperature • F

	J	F	M	A	M	J	J	A	S	O	N	D
Temperature (degs F)	76	76	73	74	80	80	80	80	80	79	79	77
Precipitation (inches)	2.6	1.1	1.3	1.4	2.3	4.4	5.8	5.8	6.7	7.0	8.0	13.8

50 Wethersfield, Connecticut

Climograph Number 2.

Precipation (inches)

Temperature ° F

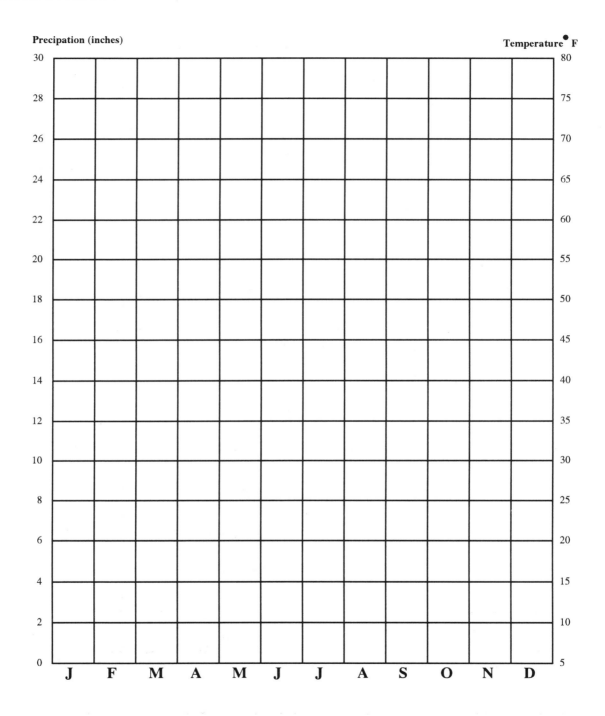

	J	F	M	A	M	J	J	A	S	O	N	D
Temperature (degs F)	25	27	36	48	58	68	73	70	63	53	41	28
Precipation (inches)	3.3	3.2	3.8	3.8	3.5	3.5	3.4	3.9	3.6	3.0	4.3	4.1

The data for Climograph No. 2 has been collected for another location in the story. Plot the data on the blank Climograph No. 2.

Compare the two charts and consider the following statements: 1) the farther north of the equator, the colder the winters, 2) the closer to the equator, the more constant the temperature, and there will be fewer and fewer extremely hot or cold days.

A. Which graph represents Wethersfield and which represents Barbados? You may want to consult a map of the world before deciding on your answer, or you may consider the data you collected for question 6.

Blank Climograph Number 3.

B. Gather temperature and precipitation data for your area from your library or Chamber of Commerce or the nearest National Weather Service Office. With that information, construct a climograph for your town (see page 52).

Comparison Chart.

8. Compare the impact of climate on the items listed on the chart below.

	In Wethersfield	In Barbados	In Your Town
Crops			
Clothing			
Recreation			
Housing			
Energy Use			

9. The residents of Wethersfield are proud of the historical setting in which they live. For many years they have researched documents related to the early years of the town and collected available records and stories from early residents. Old buildings have been marked and their histories are readily available to visitors. Some have been restored and are open to the public. An active historical society gives tours, lectures, and provides information to those who are interested in the town.

Use the resources of your school and public library to investigate the history of your own town. Are there historic buildings open to visitors? Does an historical association exist that can provide information? Can tours be arranged for young people who are interested in the history of their town? What tales are told about the people who once lived there?

Blank Climograph Number 3.

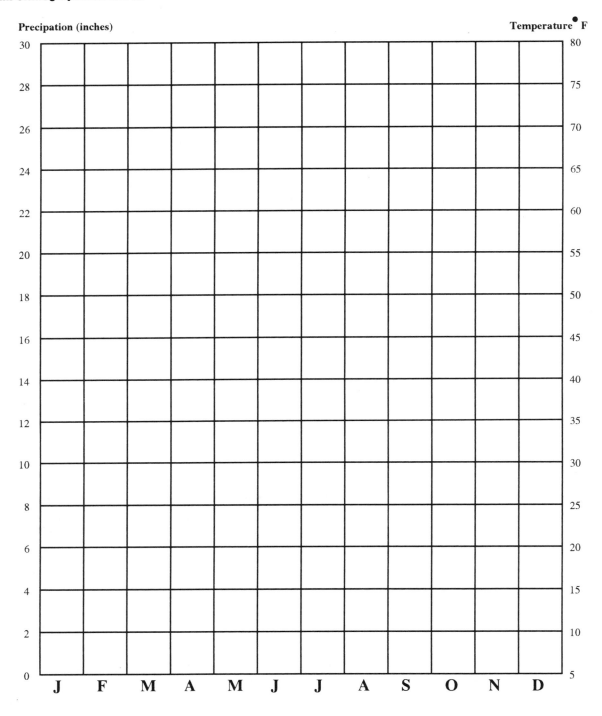

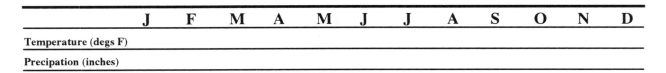

Temperature (degs F)

Precipation (inches)

10. The word *Connecticut* comes from the Mohegan Indian word *Quinnehtukgut*, meaning "long, tidal river." Use reference materials in your school or public library to discover the origin of the name of your state. Among the many books providing information on state names are:

Arnold, Pauline, and Percival White. *How We Named Our States.* New York: Harper & Row, 1966.

Kane, Joseph Nathan. *Facts About the States.* New York: H. W. Wilson, 1989.

Shearer, Benjamin, and Barbara Shearer. *State Names, Seals, Flags, and Symbols.* New York: Greenwood, 1987.

Discussion Questions

The Witch of Blackbird Pond has been criticized for copping out on feminist issues. While Kit is praised for her "independent spirit, her rejection of bigoted values, and her truly striking courage at a time when women were burned for witchcraft, . . . the book is marred only by the plot's revolving around the standard question: "Whom shall Kit marry?" (The Feminists on Children's Literature. "A Feminist Look at Children's Books." *School Library Journal* 17, no. 5 [January 1971]: 19-24).

However, other critics have defended the novel, asserting that in seventeenth-century Connecticut, girls had little choice except to find a suitable man to support them, so the question of whom they would marry was all important. This view holds that the emphasis on finding a partner is part of the novel's authenticity (Apseloff, Marilyn Fain. *Elizabeth George Speare*, p. 62. New York: Twayne, 1991). Discuss both viewpoints of the book, and discuss the choices Kit considered in the last chapter of the book. How would those choices have been different today?

For Further Reading

Other Books by Elizabeth George Speare

The Bronze Bow. Boston: Houghton Mifflin, 1961. 254 pages.
   Daniel is an angry young Palestinian whose father was murdered by Romans occupying his homeland. He is filled with hatred and longs for a revolt against the Romans. When he meets Jesus and hears his message, Daniel begins to realize that power is better gained through love, not hatred.

Calico Captive. Boston: Houghton Mifflin, 1957. 272 pages.
   This story is based on the real capture of a New Hampshire family by a Native American in the 1750s. The adventure is seen through the eyes of 14-year-old Miriam, who, along with her older sister and her sister's family, is held for four years. The French and Indians are allies in a war against the British, and the captives are forced to walk first to an Indian camp and then to the French city of Montreal, where the Indians plan to sell them.

Life in Colonial America. New York: Random House, 1963. 172 pages.
Details of everyday life are told in an interesting, enthusiastic style unusual in a book of nonfiction. This book is useful as a companion to Speare's historical novels, for there are many references to elements found in those stories, like the witchcraft fever that gripped New England.

The Sign of the Beaver. Boston: Houghton Mifflin, 1983. 135 pages.
The year is 1768, and Matt is 13 when his father leaves him alone in the Maine wilderness. The two have built a cabin and planted crops, and now Matt is in charge while his father returns to Massachusetts for the rest of the family. Matt faces starvation when he loses both his food stores and his gun. Then he is befriended by an indian chief and his grandson.

About Elizabeth George Speare

Apseloff, Marilyn Fain. *Elizabeth George Speare.* New York: Twayne, 1991.
This well-researched and carefully documented look at the life and work of Elizabeth George Speare provides the most complete biographical information on Speare available, and includes a detailed examination of her published work.

Barbados

Broberg, Merle. *Barbados.* New York: Chelsea House, 1989. 95 pages.
In this survey, the topography, people, and culture of the island are introduced.

Colonial Life

D'Amato, Janet, and Alex D'Amato. *Colonial Crafts for You to Make.* New York: Messner, 1975. 64 pages.

_____. *More Colonial Crafts for You to Make.* New York: Messner, 1975. 64 pages.
Gives instructions for making replicas of colonial buildings, rooms, and tools, and techniques for creating samples of the arts and crafts of the period.

Earle, Alice Morse. *Home Life in Colonial Days.* 1898. Reprint. Middle Village, NY: Jonathon David Publisher, 1975. 470 pages.
This detailed and exhaustive resource accurately describes various facets of daily life in the early years of America. Of special interest to readers of *The Witch of Blackbird Pond* are the chapters on flax and wool culture and spinning, girls' occupations, colonial dress, Sunday in the colonies, and colonial neighborliness. Authentic articles used in the past, now considered antiques, have been identified and described.

Glubok, Shirley, ed. *Home and Child Life in Colonial Days.* New York: Macmillan, 1969. 357 pages.
This is an abridgement of Earle's *Home Life in Colonial Days* and *Child Life in Colonial Days,* carefully edited and illustrated with new photographs. Especially interesting are the chapters on education, school books, story and picture books, games, pastimes, and toys.

Hawke, David Freeman. *Everyday Life in Early America.* New York: Harper & Row, 1988. 195 pages.

People of seventeenth-century America are presented in vivid detail. Included are photos of death's-head tombstones in the Wethersfield ancient burial ground. Many aspects of everyday life are presented from an understanding and sympathetic viewpoint.

Hoople, Cheryl G. *The Heritage Sampler: A Book of Colonial Arts and Crafts.* New York: Dial, 1975. 132 pages.

Do you want more information on that husking bee that Kit and Judith attended and on the significance of finding the red ear of corn? The answers are in this interesting book with other entertaining information on colonial foods and activities, with instructions on how to do them yourself.

Penner, Lucille Recht. *The Colonial Cookbook.* New York: Hastings House, 1976. 128 pages.

The first colonists took the raw ingredients they found in their new land, learned Indian cooking methods, and then created their own adaptations of meals they knew in Europe. Here are 49 of those dishes along with interesting notes and illustrations taken from period prints and photos of the furniture and cooking implements of the time.

Perl, Lila. *Slumps, Grunts, and Snickerdoodles: What Colonial America Ate and Why.* New York: Seabury, 1975. 125 pages.

The treasure here is not only the 13 authentic recipes, but the historical background and fascinating stories behind them.

Smith, Carter, ed. *Daily Life: A Sourcebook on Colonial America.* Brookfield, CT: Millbrook Press, 1991. 96 pages.

This book opens with an interesting timeline of the major events from the years 1490 to 1799. The strength of the book is the many illustrations taken from the collections of the Library of Congress that show daily colonial life through images produced at the time.

_____. *Governing and Teaching: A Sourcebook on Colonial America.* Brookfield, CT: Millbrook Press, 1991. 96 pages.

This well-illustrated study is limited to the historical, political, and religious aspects of the Colonies.

Tunis, Edwin. *Colonial Living.* New York: Crowell, 1976. 155 pages.

This is a detailed description of common objects of everyday life in the colonies from 1564 to 1770. Costumes, buildings, and useful items are shown as they were used in those times and places.

Colonial Witchcraft Fears (Fiction)

Clapp, Patricia. *Witches' Children*. New York: Lothrop, Lee & Shepard, 1982. 160 pages.
   This is Tituba's story told from the point of view of one of her accusers. (See Petry below.)

Farber, Norma. *Mercy Short: A Winter Journal. North Boston, 1692-93*. New York: Dutton, 1982. 138 pages.
   Mercy had been a captive of the Indians, but now is a servant in Boston, plagued by memories. Puritan Cotton Mather is called upon to cure her of demons.

Minshull, Evelyn. *The Dune Witch*. Philadelphia: Westminster Press, 1972. 159 pages.
   The Puritan settlers are afraid of the wild new land and the dangers they face, so they blame their troubles on witchcraft. Young Priss Whittenay is horrified when she is the one they accuse.

Petry, Ann. *Tituba of Salem Village*. New York: Crowell Jr. Books, 1964. 254 pages.
   Tituba and her husband, who had been slaves in Barbados, are owned by a minister who moved to Salem. There Tituba is accused of witchcraft and brought to trial.

Rinaldi, Ann. *A Break with Charity*. New York: Harcourt, 1992. 256 pages.
   This is a blend of fact and fiction about the Salem witchcraft trials. In a revealing "Author's Note," Rinaldi explains how she wove historical figures and events together with her own imagination to create this taut, enthralling novel. A bibliography of sources is appended.

Smith, Claude Clayton. *The Stratford Devil*. New York: Walker, 1984. 192 pages.
   This tragic tale reveals much about the values and motivations of the Puritans. It is based on the true story of the hanging of a young woman as witch in Stratford, Connecticut, somewhat before the period of *The Witch of Blackbird Pond*.

Connecticut

Kent, Deborah. *America the Beautiful: Connecticut*. Chicago: Children's Press, 1990. 144 pages.
   The history, government, economy, geography, industry, famous people, and important sites of Connecticut are introduced in clear text with numerous photos, maps, and drawings. An appendix of charts, graphs, and maps, and an extensive index make this a good reference source.

Roth, David M. *Connecticut: A Bicentennial History*. New York: W.W. Norton, 1979. 231 pages.
   The chapter on colonial Connecticut gives an especially insightful look at Puritan life and the conflict with the Quakers.

Soderlind, Arthur E. *Colonial Connecticut*. New York: Nelson, 1976.
   A clear picture of Puritan life and early Wethersfield is included in this history of Connecticut from its exploration to 1788.

Quakers

Elgin, Kathleen. *The Quakers: The Religious Society of Friends.* New York: McKay, 1968.
This is a comprehensive look at the history of the sect; how it was founded, and how it grew and developed in America; and how it functions in contemporary society. The stories of famous Quakers are told and questions about the faith are answered.

Seafaring Adventure

Avi. *The True Confessions of Charlotte Doyle.* New York: Franklin Watts, 1990. 224 pages.
Thirteen-year-old Charlotte is traveling across the Atlantic on a ship bound for Rhode Island in 1832. The captain is going mad, the crew is mutinous, and Charlotte must decide with whom to cast her lot.

Witches

Jackson, Shirley. *The Witchcraft of Salem Village.* New York: Random House, 1987. 146 pages.
This is a simple account of the infamous witchcraft trials that resulted in the hanging of 20 people. A difficult subject is treated clearly and without sensationalism.

Zeinert, Karen. *The Salem Witchcraft Trials.* New York: Watts, 1989. 95 pages.
The emphasis here is on explaining how the hysteria could have begun and then grown out of control.

3

Crisfield, Maryland

The Setting for Cynthia Voigt's

Homecoming
Atheneum, 1981. 312 pages.

Dicey's Song
Atheneum, 1982. 196 pages.

A Solitary Blue
Atheneum, 1983. 189 pages.

The Runner
Atheneum, 1985. 181 pages.

Come a Stranger
Atheneum, 1986. 190 pages.

Sons from Afar
Atheneum, 1987. 224 pages.

Seventeen Against the Dealer
Atheneum, 1989. 192 pages.

Book Summaries

Homecoming

It is late spring when the four Tillerman children find themselves abandoned in the parking lot of a large shopping mall in Connecticut. Thirteen-year-old Dicey, the oldest and most responsible of the children, tries to piece together the events that have led them to this point of desperation. Momma had awakened them in the middle of the night and told them they were all leaving to go to her Aunt Cilla's in Bridgeport. They packed a few clothes in paper bags and drove off in their old car, leaving the small cabin in the dunes outside of Provincetown, Massachusetts, with their rent long overdue. Dicey read the map for her mother, finding roads with no tolls. Momma pulled into the mall parking lot this morning and instructed the younger children to mind Dicey. Then she got out of the car and walked into the mall. She never returned.

Now they are alone: James, who is 10, intensely serious, and good in school; shy, quiet, nine-year-old Maybeth; Sammy, who is six, but strong for his age and very stubborn; and Dicey, who is always expected to be the responsible one.

Dicey doesn't want to admit that Momma would just walk off and leave them, but she had been acting strange lately. There had been little or no money since their father left several years ago, and none since her mother had lost her job. Now they were on the way to a great aunt that none of the children had ever seen and only knew about through Christmas cards. But Momma had written the Bridgeport address on their clothes bags and made Dicey memorize it. Now Dicey, fearing that they might be put into an orphanage and separated if they are discovered by the authorities, determines to take the children to Bridgeport in any way she can, even if it means walking all the way. They have almost no money, but they do have their health, their love and loyalty to each other, and Dicey's capability, cleverness, and determination.

As they begin their journey, the children look back to see the police pull up to their empty car and examine its contents. Dicey knows her decision to leave and find their way to Bridgeport has been the right one. It isn't very long before the children realize the task they have undertaken is almost impossible.

They walk the hot, noisy, and congested U.S. Highway 1, finding shelter in vacant buildings, parks, and at the edges of lonely roads. With little money, food is scarce, and when it is available it is carefully rationed. Dicey earns a bit from time to time doing odd jobs, and they fish when they can, but hunger is soon a constant companion. Strength of character and strong values are illustrated by Dicey's refusal to resort to any type of thievery to feed her family. Several times, Dicey feels they can go no farther, but somehow they manage to overcome obstacles and struggle on. Evenings spent around campfires, singing the folksongs Momma taught them, restore the family's flagging spirits.

After weeks on the road, they reach New Haven where they take refuge from a driving rain by huddling in some bushes on the green at Yale University. They are discovered by a college student who feeds them, gives them shelter, and then drives them to Bridgeport. They find Aunt Cilla's house, but learn from her spinster daughter that she is dead.

Middle-aged, fussy Cousin Eunice reluctantly takes the children in and asks her parish priest for advice. He contacts the authorities who locate Momma in a state mental hospital in Massachusetts. She is catatonic, and there is little or no hope of recovery. Throughout the series, Dicey and James continue to worry about their mother's "craziness," fearful that it might be hereditary, a danger either to themselves or to Maybeth. Cousin Eunice recalls that her mother was born in Crisfield, a small town on Maryland's Eastern Shore, so Father Joseph makes inquiries there and discovers that the children have a widowed grandmother, a recluse named Abigail Tillerman. He tells Dicey that their mother ran away with their father, a merchant seaman named Francis Verricker, when she was 21.

Although Cousin Eunice agrees to provide for the Tillermans, they don't fit into her plans nor do they fit into the activities that she and Father Joseph arrange for them. Sammy is labeled a troublemaker at the boy's summer camp and Maybeth is suspected of being "slow." But James excels at the Catholic priest's summer academy. Uneasy about her charges, Dicey secretly takes a part-time job and hoards away all her earnings. By mid-summer she is determined to go to Crisfield by herself to see if they can make a home with their grandmother. James discovers her plan and insists that they all make the journey to Crisfield.

Dicey thinks she has enough money saved to take them all to the Eastern Shore of Maryland on a bus, but she is fearful that Aunt Eunice will send the police to track them down. To avoid possible discovery, they take a bus to Annapolis, Maryland, planning to travel on their own the rest of the way.

The trip becomes dangerous when the children agree to work as pickers for a mercenary farmer, Mr. Rudyard, who tries to capture them and claim they are his foster children. They escape and flee cross-country with the farmer in pursuit. They are rescued by the owner of a small circus who befriends them and allows them to stay with the circus until it reaches Crisfield.

Far from welcoming their arrival, Abigail Tillerman tells Dicey they cannot stay with her, even though her remote, weather-beaten house on the run-down farm is more than large enough for all of them. She agrees, however, to take them in temporarily. Fiercely independent, private, and proud, Abigail has shunned all contact with the world since the death of her overbearing, cruel husband and her youngest son Bullet, who was killed in Vietnam. Although she lives in poverty, she refuses to apply for Social Security, disdaining "welfare."

Once again, Dicey's determination and resourcefulness serve the Tillerman children well as she strives to change this prickly old woman's mind and make a home for her family with their grandmother.

In 1981, *Homecoming* was nominated for the American Book Award and was selected as a Notable Children's Trade Book in the Field of Social Studies by the Joint Committee of the National Council for Social Studies and the Children's Book Council in the same year. It was also selected as one of "The Best of the Best Books for Young Adults" by the American Library Association and named a New York Times Outstanding Book in 1981.

Dicey's Song

This sequel begins almost immediately after the concluding events in *Homecoming*, when Gram has determined that the Tillerman children must stay with her, and that she will make the arrangement permanent through legal adoption. The children and Gram are learning to be a family. Sammy tries very hard to be good, but is often quite unsuccessful. Maybeth, still painfully shy, cannot seem to overcome her reading handicap but proves to be something of a musical prodigy and takes joy learning homemaking skills. Her music teacher, Mr. Lingerle, becomes a valued family friend. James is an outstanding student, loves books and ideas, but longs to be popular. Dicey still feels a strong responsibility for her family and is constantly hatching plans to help them. She is bored at school, with the teachers and with the other students, and they largely ignore her. Gram has given herself to the task of providing a home for her grandchildren, but is still wary of opening old wounds or risking new ones.

Almost against her will, Dicey makes two friends: Minna Smiths, the intelligent, strong, and popular daughter of a black minister; and Jeff Greene, who, like Dicey, is a solitary, independent sort who enjoys music.

During all of *Homecoming* and most of *Dicey's Song* the Tillermans long to have their Momma back with them, but in the end Gram and Dicey travel to Boston to be there, heartbroken but resigned, when Momma dies. They bring her ashes home to Crisfield so that she can be buried under the paper mulberry tree in front of the house. The book closes with the family, tight-knit and loyal, comforting one another.

Dicey's Song received the Newbery Medal in 1983 and was a *Boston Globe-Horn Book* Honor Book that same year. It was selected as one of the American Library Association's Notable Children's Books in 1982.

A Solitary Blue

Jeff Greene's story opens in Baltimore, Maryland, where his father is a history professor at a large college. Like Dicey, he was abandoned by his mother, but for very different reasons. Melody Greene is long on charm but lacks maturity and responsibility and is more concerned with saving the world than recognizing and fulfilling the needs of her son and husband. Jeff is only seven years old when his mother leaves him and his father, a remote, scholarly professor, to become a social and environmental activist. Jeff reacts by striving to please his father, fearing he will leave too, and the two go about their lives pretending nothing has happened. The next five years are empty ones for Jeff, with no word from Melody and an increasing sense of distance from his father. It is only when a serious bout with pneumonia brings Jeff to his father's attention that the gulf between them begins to narrow.

At that time, Jeff's mother re-enters his life. He spends two summers with her in Charleston, South Carolina, where he meets a great-grandmother who is living in decaying splendor among treasures from a wealthy past. During those summers, Jeff learns to love music and to play the guitar but is repeatedly betrayed by Melody, who is now revealed as totally false. Jeff begins to think of himself as the solitary blue heron he has seen on the coastal islands and nears a mental breakdown before his father and a close family friend, Brother Thomas, recognize the danger and step in to help. Only then does Jeff begin to understand how much his mother has hurt him and his father.

Professor Greene, Jeff's father, publishes a successful book, bringing a modest financial gain, and Jeff and his father look for a new home that will take them away from the stresses of Baltimore and allow Jeff the space to heal. They finally find a waterfront cabin just outside Crisfield, which they purchase and remodel. The growing closeness between Jeff and his father and his own emotional development bring Jeff a new self-confidence and strength. When he meets Dicey Tillerman, Jeff is already well on the way to recovery. Practical and responsible Dicey is the antithesis of the childlike, selfish, and treacherous Melody, and Jeff is attracted by that difference.

Several fascinating scenes are repeated from *Dicey's Song*, but this time from Jeff's point of view and with the Tillermans as supporting players.

The book ends with a final confrontation with Melody during which Jeff feels nothing but pity for her and relief when she is gone.

A Solitary Blue was both a *Newbery Honor Book* and *Boston Globe-Horn Book* Honor Book in 1984. It was named as both a "Notable Children's Book" and a "Best Book for Young Adults" by the American Library Association that same year, and it received the Parents' Choice Award in 1983.

The Runner

This book in the Tillerman series jumps back a generation and readers of *Homecoming* and *Dicey's Song* know at the outset what becomes of the main character. The year is 1967 and 17-year-old Samuel "Bullet" Tillerman is a loner who runs 10 miles every day. Dicey's mother, Liza, is Bullet's older sister, and she and older brother John have already been driven from home by their cold, tyrannical father. Bullet's mother, Abigail, seems to be the only person who loves and understands him, although her subservient relationship with her despotic husband keeps her from openly supporting her son. Bullet despises his father and is silent, defiant, and unyielding in his relationship with him. When his father orders him to get a haircut, Bullet has his head shaved.

The angry young man scorns his classmates because they don't see themselves honestly or share his drive to always do his best. Bullet is a natural athlete who never gives in, and he always wins at cross-country, his only sport. He is the star of the team, but has no respect for the coach and avoids any contact with the other runners.

In an era when racism is emerging as a national issue, Bullet is a bigot. He hates "coloreds" and refuses to help in the training of a talented and intelligent black runner, Tamer Shipp, who is new on the cross-country team. Bullet is shocked when he finds out that the waterman, Patrice, his respected friend and after school employer, is part black.

When he realizes that Tamer is another person who always works to be the best he can be, Bullet learns that a person's worth depends on character, not color.

Bullet pities his older sister, and part of his anger with his father is because vulnerable, beautiful Liza felt forced to leave home and has never returned or written. In a compelling episode, Frank Verricker, the man Liza ran away with, returns briefly to Crisfield in the company of a new girlfriend. He shows Bullet a picture of Liza holding a dark-haired, serious little girl named Dicey. Frank says that Dicey is his daughter, although he claims that Liza will not marry him. The incident serves to add fuel to Bullet's anger at the world.

After a brilliant performance at the state track and field meet in Frederick, Maryland, during which he leads his team to the state title, Bullet sees his mother withdrawing from the crowd of spectators. He knows she has made the long bus trip to see him run, but his victory is not mentioned by his parents, that day or ever.

Bullet enlists in the Army on his 18th birthday to be free of his father. The book ends with his mother's violent anguish when she learns of his battlefield death in Vietnam.

The Runner was named a "Best Book for Young Adults" by the American Library Association.

Come a Stranger

This is the story of Mina Smiths, the strong, intelligent black girl who first appeared as Dicey's advocate and friend in *Dicey's Song*. This book spans time before, during, and after the years of those books. Ten-year-old Mina, part of a loving, close-knit minister's family, yearns to be a ballerina and is overjoyed when she wins a scholarship to a summer dance camp in Connecticut. She is the only black at the school, and when she returns home at the end of the summer she begins to question her blackness. She straightens her hair, makes friends with white classmates, and generally avoids her own background, adopting white culture instead.

The next summer, brimming with ambition, Mina eagerly returns to the camp where she finds that her fellow students and the faculty have changed their attitude toward her. Now viewed as an outsider, she is told her body has grown too awkward for ballet, and Mina, heartbroken and despairing, leaves the camp. Tamer Shipp, a young black pastor who is temporarily based at her father's church in Crisfield, drives Mina home. Tamer, who was Bullet's teammate in *The Runner*, is married to a pretty but sad wife and has several small children. Nevertheless, Mina falls in love with him, well aware that her feelings are not returned.

Once again, episodes from previous Tillerman novels are replayed, this time through Mina's eyes, and another part of the family saga is filled in. Mina's mother is a nurse, a student of history, and an extremely intelligent and strong woman. It is she, more than anyone else, who provides the solid foundation that allows Mina to grow in strength, integrity, and independence.

Mina learns of Tamer's admiration for Bullet and his grief over his death in Vietnam. The climax of the story comes when she arranges for his meeting with the Tillermans, which brings some peace to him and to Abigail.

Come a Stranger ends with Jeff's graduation from Crisfield High School. There Mina is introduced to Dexter Halloway, whose father teaches with Professor Greene. Dexter's family hopes to move to Crisfield, and Mina has high hopes for a future that might include this new friend.

Come a Stranger won the Judy Lopez Award in 1987.

Sons from Afar

It has been six years since the Tillerman children arrived in Crisfield to live with their grandmother. Dicey is away at college, learning, making friends, and growing up. The rest of the family is at home. James, who is trying to figure out if he.is a "dork" and why he doesn't fit in with the rest of the high school crowd, decides it would help him to understand himself if he knew more about their father. He enlists Sammy's help, and together they begin the investigation.

The action of the story is played out alternating between each boy's point of view, and each of them secretly feels his own faults may be inherited from their long-lost father.

Frank Verricker, their father, was born in Cambridge, Connecticut, a small town north of Crisfield. James and Sammy arrange a day trip to Cambridge and talk to two teachers who knew the young Frankie. From the teachers the boys learn of Frank's family background and that, although he was smart and had a lot of potential, he was a manipulator, a liar, and probably a thief.

James decides to try to find out more information in the Hall of Records in Annapolis, Maryland, so he signs up for a class fieldtrip to the state capital. He gets a job as a part-time office clerk for a pair of Crisfield doctors to earn money for the trip.

Because James has taken a job, Sammy will be alone in the crabbing business the boys have shared in past summers. He studies his friends with an eye to finding a hard-working and dependable partner for the summer, and finally decides upon a new boy in town. Robin is considered a sort of sissy by the other boys, but Sammy finds him an interesting and understanding friend.

In Annapolis, James manages to elude the guided tour arranged for his class and has the day for his own pursuits, but his investigation proves fruitless, and he returns home hopeless and frustrated.

It is Sammy who suggests the trip to Baltimore, Maryland, where seamen are hired to work on boats, to continue their investigation. He makes all the arrangements for the trip, which turns into a dangerous, frightening adventure in a run-down waterfront bar.

The little the boys manage to unearth about their father is not reassuring, and they decide he is not worth further concern. However, their joint search and analysis has led to an understanding of themselves and of each other.

Sons from Afar was named one of the "Best Books for Young Adults" by the American Library Association.

Seventeen Against the Dealer

Dicey is 21 now and has left college to learn all she can about boat-building. With determination and hard work, she has saved enough money to begin her own boatyard business, rent a shop building, buy some tools, and open a bank account. She wants to build sailboats, but for now she is content to repair and provide winter storage for dinghies.

James is a pre-med student at Princeton on a full scholarship, while Maybeth and Sammy are still at home, growing and pursuing their own interests. Jeff Greene is in college too, and he and Dicey plan to marry as soon as she fulfills her dream of being a master builder of sailing craft. Throughout the novel, familiar friends are reintroduced and their current activities are revealed.

The action of the story takes place between New Year's and Valentine's Day, and during that time, because of her youthful independence, dogged determination, and pride, Dicey nearly loses everything she holds most dear. Through inexperience, she makes several serious business blunders and tries to repair the errors by working obsessively, gradually distancing herself from her family and from Jeff.

When a charming, smooth-talking, drifter appears at her shop and offers his help free of charge, Dicey is suspicious but doesn't refuse. She likes Cisco and gradually learns to trust him and so is duped when he walks off with her first big earnings. Sharp-eyed readers will rush to *Sons from Afar* and *The Runner* to compare Cisco to Frank Verricker and will be tantalized with the obvious similarities both in personality and physical description. Is Cisco actually the Tillermans long-lost father? While Voigt leaves the answer uncertain, she indicated in an interview that he was.[1]

Her overwhelming involvement in her work has kept Dicey from realizing that Gram is seriously ill and that Jeff has become remote. Jerked back to reality in the nick of time, Dicey reassesses her goals and is able to save those vital relationships. Dicey has learned that determination and hard work don't overcome all obstacles, and that she'll have to start again, but with a different perspective and a new set of goals.

About the Author

Far from the tumultuous childhoods she often depicts in her novels, Cynthia Voigt says her early years were very close to perfect, with family love and space to make mistakes. On February 25, 1942, she was born Cynthia Irving in Boston, Massachusetts, but her childhood was spent in rural southern Connecticut "in houses surrounded by spacious lawns."[2] She had two older sisters and twin brothers, 13 years her junior. Her mother recalls that "she was a straight-haired, plump, little bookworm . . . the library has always been her haven and her joy."[3]

Cynthia attended a private girls boarding school, Dana Hall in Wellesley, Massachusetts, where she was president of her senior class, a member of the Cum Laude Society, and graduated with distinction. She next attended Smith College in Northampton, Massachusetts, where she took several creative writing classes that she considered of little use, although she knew since ninth grade that she wanted to be a writer. After graduating from Smith, Cynthia moved to New York City, where she worked for the J. Walter Thompson advertising agency in public relations.

In 1964, Cynthia married and moved to Santa Fe, New Mexico, where her husband was a college student. While living there, she attended St. Michael's College to obtain a teaching certificate. The couple moved to Annapolis where their daughter Jessica was born and where Cynthia began her teaching career as a high school English teacher in Glen Burnie, Maryland. The marriage ended in divorce at about that time, and Cynthia began writing again, devoting an hour at the end of each day to it.

After three years she began teaching at the Key School in Annapolis, where she taught second-, fifth-, and seventh-grade English. During this time, Cynthia discovered the rich world of children's novels as she read and taught the best books available for young people.

In 1974, Cynthia married Walter Voigt, who also taught at the Key School. Her husband taught the classics: Greek, Latin, and ancient history. Cynthia continued to devote an hour each day to writing. While expecting her second child, she decided to teach only part-time and wrote the first draft of *The Callender Papers* before her son, Peter, was born. While Peter was still an infant, Cynthia taught school and wrote *Tell Me If the Lovers Are Losers*. When he was two, she began *Homecoming*. Both of her children spent part of their infancy in playpens in the rear of Cynthia's classrooms.

Cynthia Voigt was 37 when she first sold a book. It was *Homecoming*, and it had to be shortened by 200 pages before it was published. It came out in 1981 and was soon followed by *Tell Me If the Lovers Are Losers* (1982) an American Library Association Best Book for 1982, and *The Callender Papers* (1983), which won the Edgar Allan Poe Award from the Mystery Writers of America for the best juvenile mystery in 1984.

Mrs. Voigt said that when she finished *Homecoming*, she knew the Tillermans would be the subjects of another book, and she began *Dicey's Song* immediately. One book seemed to naturally lead to another, and the series grew into the seven very popular stories that comprise the Crisfield Novels.

Setting: Coastal Connecticut and Maryland

Following the Tillerman Trail

For the most part, Cynthia Voigt writes about places she knows. In fact, her modern, realistic fiction represents sort of a geographical autobiography. She says that when she creates a setting, she must draw a map to visualize the place and that she isn't adept at drawing maps. If it turns out that the thread of the story does not fit into the map she has created, she must redraw it until it accommodates what she wants to do with the plot.[4]

Voigt grew up in Connecticut and later lived for many years in Maryland, the two states that comprise the settings for *Homecoming*. Because she prefers to use realistic settings, many of the locations mentioned in the books can be found on maps with descriptions often accurately reflecting actual places. When Voigt "fictionalizes" reality, it is most frequently in terms of altering the distances between real places and renaming streets and roads.

Homecoming opens in the fictional town of Peewauket when a distraught Liza Tillerman walks away from her car filled with children and never returns. From the location described in the book, "Peewauket" appears to be the real town of Pawcatuck, Connecticut, but there is no large shopping mall in that small town of about 5,300 people.

Like the abandoned children in the fairy tale "Hansel and Gretel," which James tells to his restless younger brother and sister, the Tillerman children soon set out on their own to find a secure home. On that first hot, dusty day they walk along U.S. Highway 1 as it winds through unfriendly, urban scenery. At last, they turn off on a road that leads to Phillip's Beach and spend the night near an isolated and empty house. They have passed Stonington and, according to Dicey's calculations, have only traveled 8 to 10 miles.

While there is no "Phillip's Beach" in the area around Stonington (see fig. 3.1, page 68), there are certainly many narrow roads that lead toward the sea and lots of areas that are sparsely inhabited (see fig. 3.2, page 69).

Figure 3.1. Map of South Eastern Connecticut.

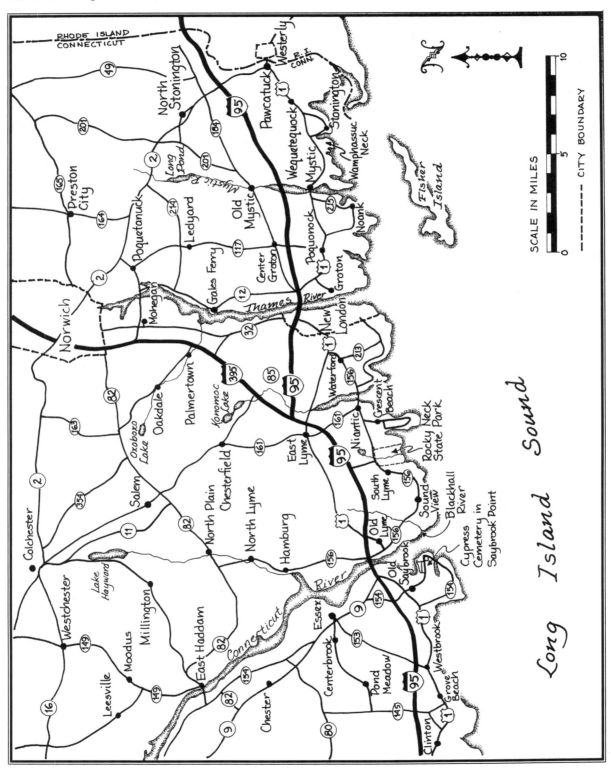

Figure 3.2. This road to Wamphassuc Neck is typical of the roads that turn off U.S. Highway 1 in southeastern Connecticut.

 The children walk the many miles to New London, Connecticut, still following U.S. Highway 1. New London figures in another book in the Tillerman series, *Come a Stranger*. It is here that Mina Smiths attends dance camp at a college built in the hills bordering the river. The location and the stately buildings and grounds of Connecticut College nicely fit the description of Mina's summer school (see fig. 3.3, page 70). Connecticut College is a small, liberal arts school for men and women with an enrollment of 1,850. Its reputation for excellence is enhanced by high entrance standards and expensive tuition.

 After they cross the Thames River, the Tillerman children turn onto a beach road that can only be State Route 156. When they are caught in rain, the hungry and tired children become cold and wet. Dicey finds protection for them in an open-sided shelter on a public beach (see fig. 3.4, page 70). There they dry their clothes and cook some food over a fire in a stone fireplace.

Figure 3.3. Connecticut College in New London.

Figure 3.4. These open-sided shelters are found at Crescent Beach just off Route 156.

The next point of refuge for the Tillermans is Rockland Park where they spend several days fishing, clamming, and resting, while James recovers from a bad fall he took climbing rocks along the seashore. The location of the park as given in the book fits the actual location of Rocky Neck State Park and the description is a close match as well (see fig. 3.5).

Figure 3.5. Map of Rocky Neck State Park.

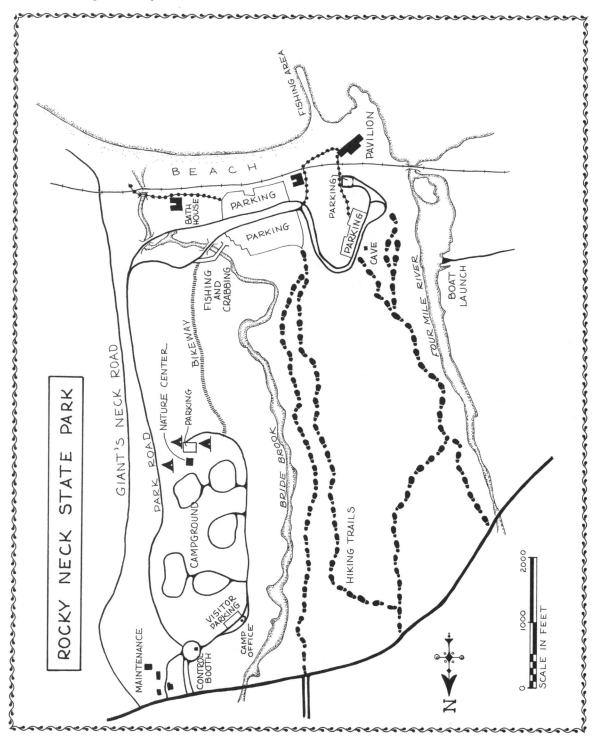

This 561-acre park is known for abundant fish, wildlife, and its scenic salt marsh, where osprey, cranes, herons, and mute swans are seasonal visitors. There are over 100 wooded and open campsites that offer accommodations and sanitary facilities.

Although the Conrail line runs along the Long Island Sound side of the park, there is a three-quarter-mile long white-sand beach with warm, clear water, and many miles of hiking trails to explore. Rocky promontories and quiet beaches are easy to find in the park (see fig. 3.6).

Figure 3.6. This camp site at Rocky Neck State Park is secluded, but not too far from the water.

Fishermen can catch mackerel, striped bass, blackfish, and flounder in the creek and marsh areas. Tradition has it that the name given to the Bride Brook (see fig. 3.7) commemorates a ceremony performed here during the winter of 1646, when Governor Winthrop stood on the east bank of the stream and united in marriage a couple standing on the opposite bank.

The Tillermans left the state park and took the road south to the town of Sound View. They spent the night camped beside a creek that emptied into the mouth of the Connecticut River. The Black Hall River is posted "Hunting and Fishing Prohibited," just as was the Tillerman's refuge the night after they left Rockland Park.

When they reached the town of Old Lyme, Dicey was stymied in her attempt to get her family across the Connecticut River. The only bridge had no walkway for pedestrians and crossing it seemed too hazardous, even for the Tillermans. While she tried to decide what to do, the children earned some money by carrying groceries for the customers of a large supermarket at the throughway entry ramp (see fig. 3.8).

Figure 3.7. In the spring, schools of alewives swim up Bride Brook to their inland spawning ground.

Figure 3.8. This supermarket can be found by following the directions given in the book. It is easy to imagine the Tillermans earning money by carrying groceries here.

After dark, the children took a rowboat they found along the shore and rowed under the bridge and downstream to a large marina at the mouth of the river (see fig. 3.9). There they tied up the boat, hoping that it would be found and returned to its owner. Later that night, the exhausted children slept in an old graveyard behind a church in a small town (see fig. 3.10). The peninsular village of Saybrook Point, with its marina and Cypress Cemetery seems to fit that description perfectly. There is a corner plot in the graveyard where the children spent the night that is identified as the first site of Yale College. The ground was given to the town in 1914 on the condition that it never be used for burials. The school, then known as the Collegiate School of Connecticut, was located here from 1707 to 1716, when it moved to New Haven. As the Collegiate School was established in Killingworth from 1702 to 1707, this might be known more accurately as the second site of the institution.

Figure 3.9. This is the part of the Connecticut River the Tillermans had to cross at night in a rowboat. This site at the river mouth was a vital British military fort in the seventeenth century.

Figure 3.10. James was correct when he speculated that this cemetery had tombstones that were hundreds of years old. Some date to the mid-seventeenth century.

For the next five days, the Tillermans followed Highway 1, spending their nights on roadsides and beaches (see fig. 3.11, page 76). One night was spent at the entrance to another state park and another in a playground beside the Branford River. The entrance to Hammonasset State Park lies on the highway taken by the Tillermans as they walked south along Long Island Sound.

Figure 3.11. Map of the south central Connecticut coastline.

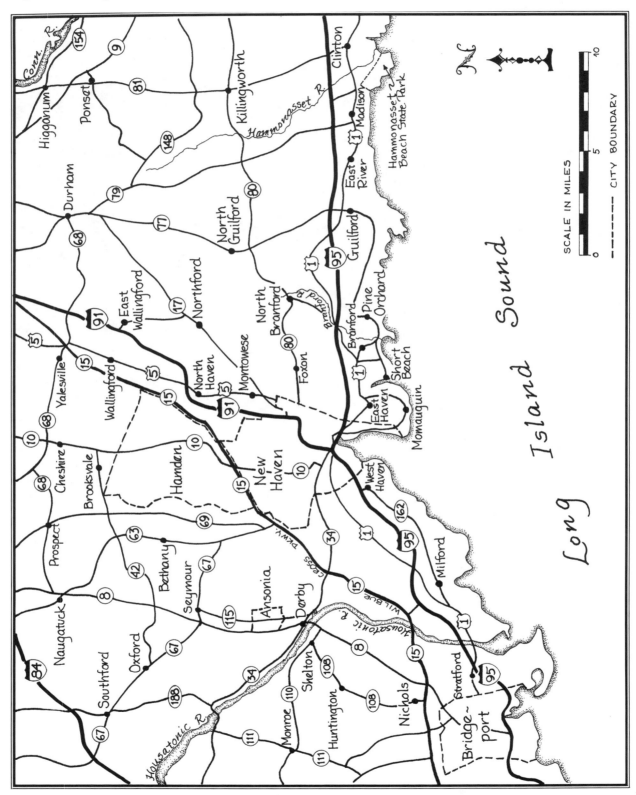

It was raining the night the children walked through New Haven. They left Highway 1 and walked up Quinnipiac Road, across Ferry Street and the Quinnipiac River, and down Chapel Street to the Yale Green in the heart of this industrial city of 130,000 residents (see fig. 3.12).

Figure 3.12. The Tillermans trudged down Chapel Street at night in a steady downpour of rain.

When the Puritan colony of New Haven was founded in 1638, it was laid out in a giant square subdivided into nine smaller squares. The center square, the green, was reserved for community use as pasture land, parade ground, and burial ground. It is still the heart of the downtown area (see fig. 3.13, page 78). Dicey sat on a bench facing the dormitories and Phelps Gate on College Street, her back to the three churches on the green that were built in the early 1800s (see fig. 3.14, page 79).

Figure 3.13. Map of Central New Haven.

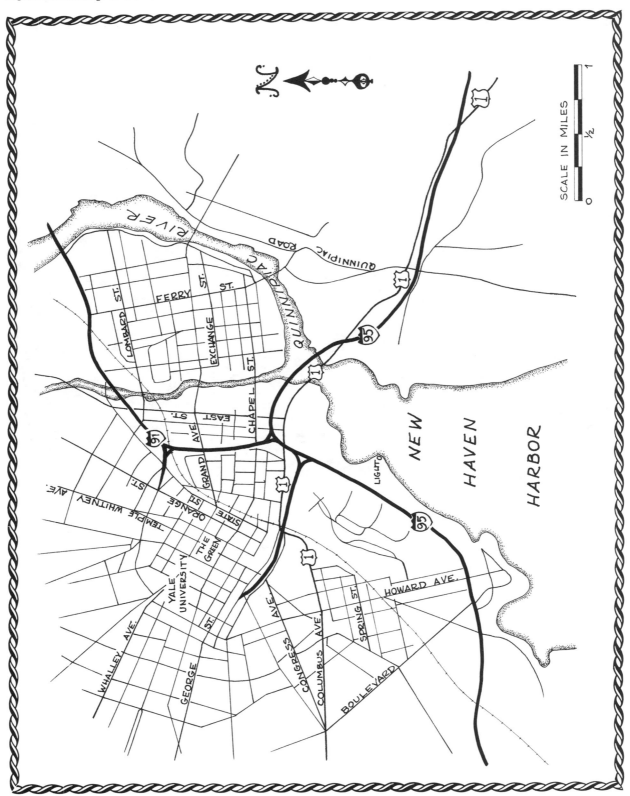

Figure 3.14. They were drenched by the time they reached the Yale Green where Dicey sat on a bench and watched over the younger children as they huddled in a cluster of bushes and tried to rest.

Yale University was given its name in 1718, after it was moved from Saybrook Point to New Haven. Today it is one of the notable educational institutions in the world. The university currently enrolls over 10,000 students in 11 graduate and professional schools and in the undergraduate college. One of Yale's outstanding attractions is the Peabody Museum, one of the world's great natural history museums. The Yale University Art Gallery is one of the finest of its type.

After their rescue by the Yale students, the Tillermans are driven to Bridgeport, traveling on the road now known as Interstate 95. Aunt Cilla's address, 1724 Ocean Drive, is fictional; there is no Ocean Drive in the large, industrial city of Bridgeport. No clues are given about the locations of the house, the church, the park, or the church camps the children attend. Bridgeport is a city that the Tillermans are eager to leave.

The bus route to Crisfield, Maryland, that Dicey initially worked out would still be usable today, but at a considerably increased fare. She expected to pay $26 for a one-way ticket from Bridgeport to Crisfield by way of New York City and Wilmington, Delaware (see fig. 3.15). Today's route would take her only to a dropoff a mile outside of Westover, Maryland, rather than all the way to Crisfield, and it would cost almost $60. She would be able to pay half fares for the other three children however, as they were all under the age of 12.

Figure 3.15. Map of east coast from Bridgeport, Connecticut, to Annapolis, Maryland, including Wilmington, Delaware.

When they arrived at the Wilmington bus terminal, Dicey discovered the bus for Salisbury left at 2:30 P.M. (it still does) and that they had missed it. Rather than wait for the next Eastern Shore bus at 9:00 P.M., she decided to leave as soon as possible on a departure bound for Annapolis. Today that change would have been impossible, for there are no direct bus routes between Wilmington and Annapolis.

Annapolis figures prominently in two of the Tillerman novels. Dicey shepherds her little family through the town in *Homecoming* and, years later, James returns to search for some record of his father in *Sons from Afar.* In *Seventeen Against the Dealer,* Dicey buys lumber at Ken's Boatyard near the Yacht Club and makes a deal to build a boat for Mr. Hobart. Because Cynthia Voigt lived in Annapolis for many years, it would be expected the city would be depicted with authenticity, and it is.

If the Tillermans were to make the bus journey to the city today, they would not arrive in the heart of Annapolis (see fig. 3.16), but at a parking lot at the Memorial Stadium off Rowe Boulevard. Then they could have taken a free shuttle bus to the downtown area.

Figure 3.16. Map of the historic area of Annapolis, Maryland.

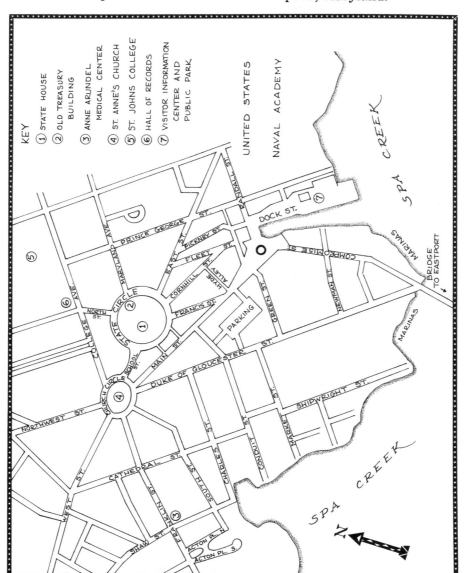

Figure 3.17. Traffic circles around St. Anne's Church just as it did when Dicey led the children around the Church.

Figure 3.18. This is the waterfront park where the Tillermans ate their ice cream cone supper in Annapolis.

Just as in *Sons from Afar*, school buses from all over Maryland arrive at the State House and students clamber off to be greeted by costumed guides who escort them through the historic area (see fig. 3.19).

St. John's College is located in the heart of Annapolis. It was on the college green that the Tillermans spent part of a summer afternoon in *Homecoming*, and James wandered in the library of St. John's in *Sons from Afar*. There are 85,000 books in the St. John's College Library and college information states that the students are "typically young people who habitually read good books." St. John's is the third oldest college in the United States and current enrollment is 417 men and women.

Figure 3.19. In *Sons from Afar,* James held the door of the State House open, but he didn't step inside to join his classmates on the tour. Instead he headed for the Hall of Records to try to find some information about his father.

When the Tillermans landed in Annapolis in *Homecoming,* they had at last arrived in Maryland. Now the problem was to cross to the Eastern Shore of Chesapeake Bay. Dicey and James cleverly talked their way into the confidence of the young crew of a small sailboat and arranged for passage (see fig. 3.20).

Figure 3.20. Sailboats hug the harbor in Annapolis.

They were put off the sailboat at the dock of the small, historic town of St. Michael, where thousands of sailboats put in each summer and near where a young black slave named Frederick Bailey was held in bondage from 1824 to 1826, and again from 1833 to 1836. Bailey later changed his name; he is better known to the world as Frederick Douglass, the abolitionist champion.

Once on shore, the children hurried down Route 33 toward the town of Easton (see fig. 3.21). They followed the same route along which Frederick Bailey (Douglass) was dragged to jail in Easton on April 2, 1836, after his attempted escape from slavery was foiled. Near Easton, they took Highway 50, going south. Dicey had decided it would be quicker to leave the road at this point and cut cross-country on dirt roads heading for the town of Salisbury (see fig. 3.22).

Figure 3.21. Map of Chesapeake Bay.

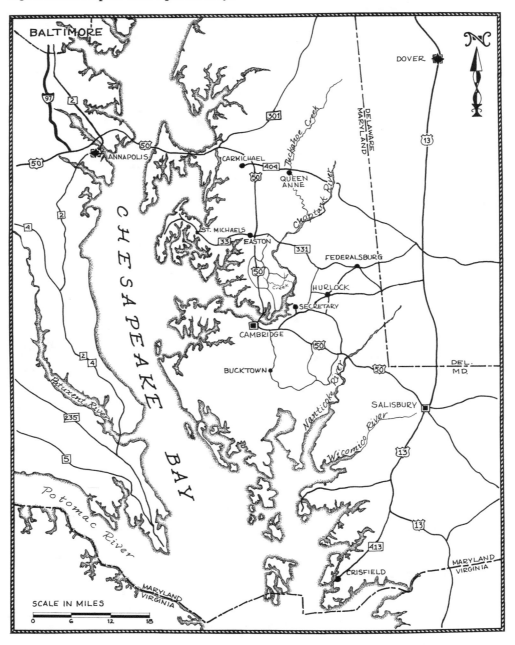

Figure 3.22. Just south of Easton, the Tillermans turned onto this road, which heads toward the Choptank River. The name of this road becomes significant in the study of Crisfield that follows.

The Tillermans camped one night on the banks of a creek that crosses the road they traveled on their way toward the Choptank. The road passes large farms as it approaches that river. It was in this area that the Tillermans nearly fell into the grip of the evil Mr. Rudyard.

The wide Choptank River (see fig. 3.23, page 86) had no bridges spanning it until 1935, so it was a cultural divide separating the Eastern Shore between rich, sophisticated landowners to the north and the isolated backwoodsmen of the south. The southern part of the Eastern Shore tends to be more conservative in politics and more fundamentalist in religion, and for many years the Choptank marked the boundary between the northern counties where liquor could be purchased and the southern counties where its sale was illegal.

When Rudyard pursued them, the Tillermans found protection with the owner of the Hawkins circus, which was performing on the grounds of the elementary school in Hurlock. The children stayed with Will Hawkins and his circus while it played in Salisbury. Then one morning, he drove them south to Crisfield.

Figure 3.23. The Choptank River where the children escaped from Rudyard.

Crisfield, Maryland

Figure 3.24. Map of Crisfield.

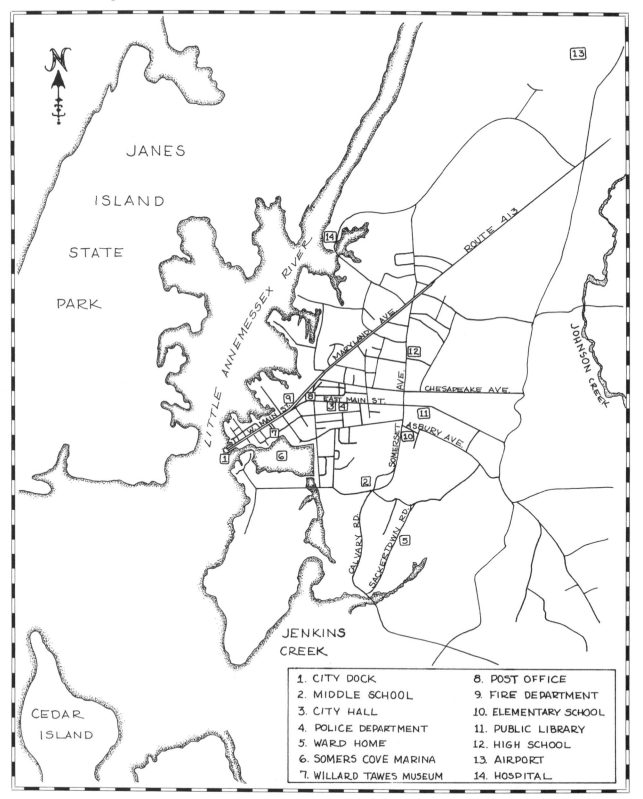

1. CITY DOCK
2. MIDDLE SCHOOL
3. CITY HALL
4. POLICE DEPARTMENT
5. WARD HOME
6. SOMERS COVE MARINA
7. WILLARD TAWES MUSEUM
8. POST OFFICE
9. FIRE DEPARTMENT
10. ELEMENTARY SCHOOL
11. PUBLIC LIBRARY
12. HIGH SCHOOL
13. AIRPORT
14. HOSPITAL

Figure 3.25. Crisfield welcome sign.

Crisfield is the primary setting for all seven of the books in the Tillerman family series, sometimes known as the Crisfield Novels. Cynthia Voigt chose the Crisfield locale because she thought it looked like the end of nowhere on a map, and when she saw the town, she knew it was the setting she wanted.

Crisfield, in Somerset County, is on an inlet of Tangier Sound, a part of Chesapeake Bay protected from the main body of water by a series of small islands. The town has a population of about 2,900 year-round residents, but that number swells in the summer as vacationers explore the area. Reputed to be the heart of the Maryland seafood industry, Crisfield is the home of several soft shell and hard shell crab-processing and shipping companies, and the Somers Cove Marina is the permanent haven for a large charter boat fleet because Tangier Sound contains some of the finest fishing grounds in Chesapeake Bay (see fig. 3.26).

Figure 3.26. The Crisfield docks and harbor serve the large local seafood industry.

Abigail Tillerman alludes to the town's colorful history when she tells James about the Crisfield fortunes that were made in oysters and crabs and also how the town became a haven for lawlessness and bootlegging. She later admits, in *Dicey's Song,* that their own family was engaged in the bootlegging trade for a while.

Crisfield does indeed have a rough-and-tumble history. The name given to the area by the Native American tribes who lived there was "Annemessex," which means "bountiful waters"—referring to the abundant food supply available in the Bay and nearby marshes and streams. Early settlers began farming in the area in the mid-seventeenth century. They came mostly from Virginia and were seeking both religious freedom and choice farmland. In 1666, Benjamin Summers settled in the area now known as Crisfield, and a small fishing village called Somers Cove grew up near his home. That village, as well as other settlements along the Eastern Shore, were plagued with raids from pirates, or "picaroons," who made their living preying on shipping in the Bay.

By 1800, there were 17,388 people living in Somerset County, and Somers Cove, the largest town, had over 100 buildings. Farmers grew wheat, corn, tobacco, and cotton, and fishing was becoming an important industry.

During the Civil War, loyalties were divided in Somers Cove. As the southernmost community in the border state of Maryland, many of the local men were Southern sympathizers and escaped the Northern draft to join the Confederate army. It was not unusual for families to have some sons fighting for the North and some for the South.

After the Civil War, the oyster industry grew quickly, and within a few years, oyster boats converged on Tangier Sound and the tributaries of Chesapeake Bay by the hundreds. The crews from these boats spent their off-hours in town, and soon the village had turned into a tough and riotous community with nearly all buildings located on or next to the waterfront.

The railroad came to Somers Cove as a result of the increase in the seafood industry. The tiny Eastern Shore Railroad had started to lay tracks to the town because it had the best deep water port in Tangier Sound. The president of the railroad, John Woodland Crisfield, who was also a financier and former Congressman, sold it to the Pennsylvania Railroad; by 1866, trains were hauling oysters directly from central Chesapeake Bay to major markets in the east and midwest. The little village, with its railroad running right down the main street to the harbor, became a metropolis for seafood, shipping millions of gallons of oysters and tons of fish, wildfowl, and clams.

To honor the man who had been influential in this rapid growth and prosperity, the town was renamed Crisfield. Local legend has it that John Crisfield, in top hat and tailcoat, fell off the gangplank at the city dock during the 1866 celebration of the completion of the rail line to the city. Mr. Crisfield couldn't swim, but was speedily rescued by two of his agents, and the townspeople decided to soothe his feelings by naming the town for him. Historians say the incident may have really happened a few years after 1866, and that the town already carried his name at the time of Crisfield's dunking.

Because of its growing importance as a seafood center, Crisfield was incorporated in 1872, and the first order of business for the new town commission was to bring law and order to the city. Until that time, there had been no jail in town. Lawbreakers were confined in a railroad boxcar until 1873, when a jail was constructed of white oak and named the "calaboose." In 1875, just as Abigail Tillerman related, the town commissioners passed an ordinance making Crisfield "dry"—no liquor could be sold in town. They closed all the taverns, and the town became law-abiding, at least on the surface. But by August 14, 1909, the local newspaper, the *Crisfield Times,* complained that "Crisfield [is] in worse condition than if open saloons were permitted," because of the number of strangers in the community selling liquor illegally. Crisfield's reputation as a wild and woolly town continued.

Still, wealth and prosperity continued to grow, and Crisfield was known as a boisterous boom town and the "Seafood Capital of the World." Oyster packers rolled shells out from the shucking houses and piled them into enormous mounds on the marsh. Later, other merchants and tradesmen leveled those mounds and built their buildings right on top of the base of oyster shells. Oyster shells, an average of six-feet deep, remain the foundation on which most of downtown Crisfield is built. Seafood packers built huge, turreted Victorian houses like those Dicey noticed on her first day in town.

The population at the turn of the century has been estimated at 11,000 to 12,000 people. By 1910, the Crisfield Customs House had the largest registry of sailing vessels of any port in the nation, and the Eastern Shore Steamship Company had begun nightly delivery service from Crisfield to Baltimore on luxurious paddle wheelers.

It was in the 1920s that the oyster supply started to dry up; soon after, trucks and airplanes took over freighting and brought to an end the railroad service that once bustled into Crisfield. Today, only the wide, divided road that leads to the dock is a reminder that once tracks ran down the center of that street.

The oyster industry almost disappeared for a while, and clams are no longer plentiful. The only item that survives in relatively large quantities is the crab, and Crisfield has developed a thriving crab-processing industry. About 26 million crabs are handled each year in a $7 million per year industry.

Today Crisfield is a quiet, peaceful little town of about 3,000 citizens that caters to tourists, especially those who bring their boats into the marina and fish the creeks and coves. Cruise ships leave the dock daily, crowded with visitors on $15 half-day trips bound for nearby Smith or Tangier Islands in Tangier Sound. Jane's Island is an undeveloped, natural seashore area accessible only by boat. Swimming and exploring are favorite activities on the isolated, sandy beaches. Assateague Island, with its wild ponies and National Seashore and Wildlife Refuge, is 40 miles away and offers driving, walking, and boat tours through the park.

The thriving seafood industry is much in evidence on the waterfront as workers keep the boatyard busy, and bushels of blue crab, flounder, and sea trout are unloaded and delivered to the 10 local processors. Even the town water tower is decorated with an enormous blue crab, and the high school athletic teams are the "Crisfield Crabbers."

Some folklorists consider Crisfield to be one of the richest centers in the United States of tall tales, whoppers, yarns, ghost stories, and true tales. In the shade of the roofed City Dock, old-timers gather to swap yarns on the "Liars Bench."

Every year since 1947, the entire area celebrates the National Hard Crab Derby and Fair on Labor Day weekend. There are crab-picking contests, crab-cooking contests, a Miss Crustacean Beauty contest, parades, fishing tournaments, fireworks, and, above all, the Hard Crab Derby itself, a race to determine the speediest crab in the world. In July, there is the Annual J. Millard Tawes Crab and Clam Bake at the Somers Cove Marina, reported to be the largest seafood festival on the Eastern Shore.

The Governor J. Millard Tawes Historical Museum at Somers Cove Marina has exhibits pertaining to the late governor, the history and development of Crisfield, and local art and folklore.

Crisfield was the home of Lem and Steve Ward, internationally known waterfowl carvers and painters. During their lifetimes they produced more than 25,000 decoys and decorative birds, which the men called "counterfeits." Lem did most of the painting, while Steve did most of the carving. Steve died in 1976, and Lem died in 1984 at the age of 88. Their home is located on Sackertown Road in Crisfield and examples of their art are found at the Tawes Museum and at the Ward Museum of Waterfowl Art in Salisbury.

There are 22 churches in the immediate Crisfield area, and 11 of those are Methodist, reflecting the influence of early missionaries who preached on the coastlines and islands of the Chesapeake Bay and converted the watermen.

There are three boat-building and repair shops in town, and Dicey would have been in good company in her business venture in *Seventeen Against the Dealer*. There are three motels, three gift shops, three art stores, four cruise ships, and seven restaurants to accommodate visitors. Two banks, one newspaper, and four real estate agencies serve the townspeople.

Just as Jeff Greene and his father found Crisfield a good place to escape the pressures of urban life, retirees and others from the north are discovering the serenity and beauty of the Eastern Shore and are relocating. Those old Victorian homes frequently described as neglected and rotting in the Tillerman books are being restored as new families move into town and return them to their former glory.

Crisfield and the Tillermans

The first place the Tillermans went in Crisfield was the dock, where small businesses crowd against the water. It was there that Dicey found Millie Tidings' grocery store and got directions to her grandmother's farm (see fig. 3.27).

Figure 3.27. Shops crowd up against the Crisfield dock.

In *Homecoming*, the directions were to take Main Street inland for a mile or a mile and a half to Landing Neck Road. Then they were to take Landing Neck past a bend in the road where there was a new little house. The next mailbox was Abigail Tillerman's. The whole trip is seven miles. There is actually no Landing Neck Road in or near Crisfield. (See note on the country road south of Easton, just off Route 50 on figure 3.22.) But the road in figure 3.28 shows what the road the children took may have been like.

Figure 3.28. This road winds south from Main Street toward Jenkins Creek.

There are other clues to the location of the Tillerman farm. It is located on a marsh that opens on the bay. It is about a quarter mile from the open water. Crabs were important to the Tillermans for their own food and as a source of income when James and Sammy started their own crabbing business in *Sons from Afar* (see fig 3.29).

There are many homes that fit the general description of the Tillermans, isolated and nestled among trees at the end of the marshes bordering the creeks and the Bay.

The paper mulberry tree is a native of eastern Asia where the bark is used to make paper and cloth. It is a tough, quick-growing tree that reaches a height of 40 feet. It is known for a round-shaped top, twisted trunks, and large, lobed, toothed leaves that are woolly underneath. The leaf shapes are varied and sometimes several different shapes may appear on the same shoot. The paper mulberry isn't very common in the United States, but is sometimes grown in eastern North America. It will grow in almost any soil as long as it has lots of sunlight.

Figure 3.29. This dock opens onto Jenkins Creek and Chesapeake Bay.

Figure 3.30. One of the first things Dicey notices about the Tillerman homestead is the large paper mulberry tree that stands next to the house. It becomes a symbol of home and family for them. In *Dicey's Song,* Mama's ashes are buried under the tree.

Figure 3.31. The Crisfield Elementary School. Soon after they arrive, James, Sammy, and Maybeth are enrolled in the Crisfield Elementary School, but Dicey goes to the junior high.

Dicey is assigned to junior high school in *Homecoming*, but in *Dicey's Song,* she attends the high school and meets Jeff Greene and Mina Smiths. Neither the Woodson Middle School nor the Crisfield Senior High School resemble the school described in *Dicey's Song.*

A clear description of Reverend Smith's church is given in *Come a Stranger,* but there is no church matching the description in the area of town where Mina would have lived. There is, however, a church on the main road leading out of town that comes close to the building Mina describes (see fig. 3.32). This church on Route 413, just outside of Crisfield, has a predominately African American congregation.

In *The Runner,* Bullet has laid out a 10-mile cross-country course that takes him down the shoreline, across fields, and through the marshlands along roads like that shown in figure 3.33.

Figure 3.32. Church on Route 413.

Figure 3.33. Narrow, unpaved lanes wind past docks and crab shanties south of town along Jenkins Creek.

Figure 3.34. A workboat with a small cabin at its bow chugs past the Crisfield docks.

Bullet journeyed to Frederick, Maryland, with his team for the state track and field competition. There they stayed at a small college and the races were held on tracks in and around the campus. Historic Frederick, with a population of 40,100, is the home of Hood College located on a 50-acre campus in the northeast section of the town (see fig. 3.35).

Figure 3.35. This is the entrance to Hood College in Frederick, Maryland, a womens' residential college with an enrollment of 1,100 undergraduate and 800 graduate students.

Figure 3.36. Blue herons, so important in *A Solitary Blue,* are common in the marshes around Crisfield.

Cambridge, Maryland

When Sammy and James search for information about their father, Frank Verricker, they head for his birthplace, Cambridge, Maryland (see page 98). They try to locate some record of him at the hospital, then at the Board of Education Building (see fig. 3.38, page 99). At last they were directed to Mrs. Rottman, who had been Frankie's third-grade teacher. From her they learned that their father had been a bright, challenging student inclined toward mischief and always in trouble at home. They also learned he had been expelled from high school, so that is where they went next. Their route through Cambridge can be followed exactly on the map of the city, as all streets and locations are given accurately in the book. At the intersection of Water and High streets there is a statue of a great blue heron by John Neal Mullican to commemorate the establishment of the Blackwater Wildlife Refuge just south of town.

Just a few miles southeast of Cambridge is the small community of Bucktown, Maryland, the birthplace and early home of Harriet Tubman. Tubman was born a slave in 1820 or 1821 on the plantation of Edward Brodas, the man who owned her parents, Harriet Greene and Benjamin Ross. In 1849, when she learned she was soon to be sold to a slave owner from the deep south, Harriet made her first escape north to freedom. With assistance and directions from a sympathetic white couple in Bucktown, she made her way to the banks of the Choptank River and, like the Tillerman children, escaped by walking all night along the banks and in the waters of that river.

During the next 11 years, Harriet Tubman returned to the area as many as 19 times, guiding over 300 slaves on the road north to freedom. A marker near Bucktown commemorates her accomplishments. Mina Smiths would have been gratified to know that such notable African American heroes as Harriet Tubman and Frederick Douglass were also natives of the Eastern Shore.

Figure 3.37. Cambridge.

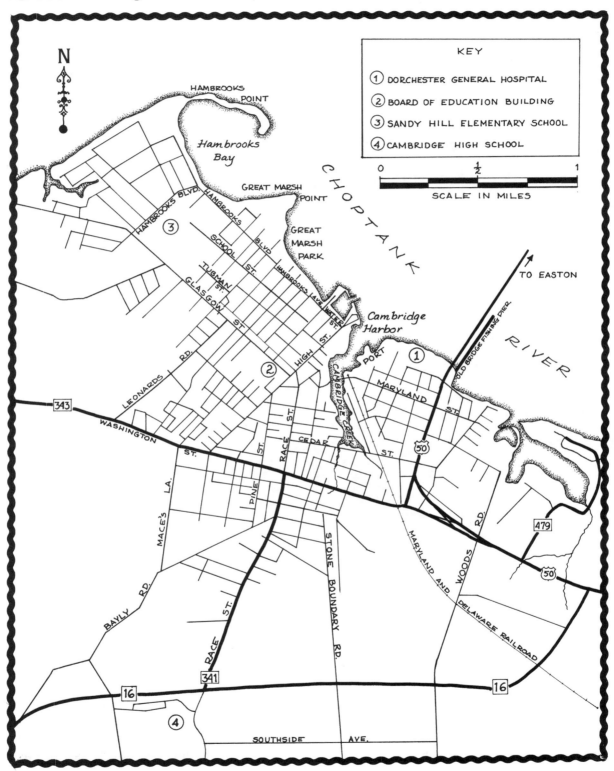

Figure 3.38. The Dorchester County Board of Education Building sits back from the street on a generous spread of lawn exactly as it is described in *Sons from Afar*.

For More Information

Crisfield Area Chamber of Commerce
9th Street
P.O. Box 292
Crisfield, MD 21817

Somerset County Library System
11767 Beechwood Street
Princess Anne, MD 21853

Notes

1. Hazel Rochman, "The Booklist Interview: Cynthia Voigt," *Booklist* 85 (April 15, 1989): 452–3.

2. Anne Commire, ed., *Something About the Author,* Vol. 48 (Detroit: Gale Research, 1987): 220.

3. Elise K. Irving, "Cynthia Voigt," *Horn Book* 59 (August 1983): 410.

4. Dorothy Kauffman, "Profile: Cynthia Voigt," *Language Arts* 62 (December 1985): 876–80.

Extended Activities

1. Using the maps on figures 3.1, 3.11, 3.15, and 3.21, begin at Pawcatuck, Connecticut, and trace the route the Tillerman children followed to Crisfield, Maryland. Be sure to consider the names of the towns and numbers of the highways given in the text of *Homecoming*.

    A. Use a blue marker to indicate the parts of the route that were traveled on foot.
    B. Use a red marker to indicate the portion of the route covered by bus.
    C. Use a yellow marker to show the parts of the trip traveled by automobile.
    D. Use a green marker to show the parts of the trip traveled by boat.

2. Using the scale of miles on the maps to calculate the following:

    A. The number of miles traveled on foot.
    B. The number of miles traveled by bus.
    C. The number of miles traveled by automobile.
    D. The number of miles traveled by boat.
    E. The total number of miles traveled in *Homecoming*.

(Hint: To measure roads with irregular curves, lay a string along the road on the map. Mark the beginning and end of the journey on the string. Next, take the string and place it along the scale of miles on the map, and calculate the number of miles represented between the beginning and ending marks on the string.)

3. Cynthia Voigt has said that the outlined plot for *Homecoming* was a series of dates and a map of red dots (Kauffman, Dorothy. "Profile: Cynthia Voigt" *Language Arts* 62 [December 1985]: 876-80).

    A. On the maps of their journey marked in question 1, place a red dot at each spot you think the children spent the night on the way from Pawcatuck to Bridgeport.
    B. Count only the days they actually moved from one location to another, and calculate the average number of miles they walked each day.
    C. Find your school on a map of your town. Now mark a spot on the map that is the same distance from your school as the average miles you calculated in B above.

4. The Tillermans traveled through two different regions of our country. Compare the city of Bridgeport where they lived with Cousin Eunice to the Crisfield area where they ended their journey. (See maps A-J following.)

    A. Use the thematic maps to prepare a chart (see page 106) that compares the Crisfield area of Maryland with Bridgeport, Connecticut. Find the same information for the region where you live and add that to the chart.

(Text continues on page 106.)

Map A—Maryland Population.

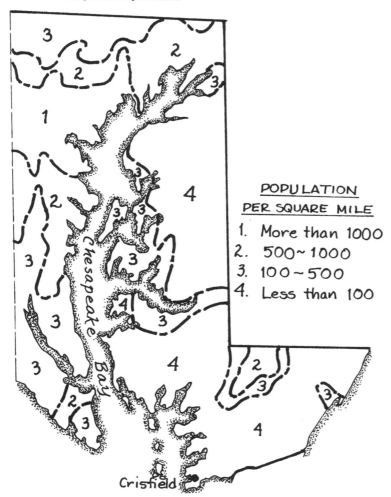

POPULATION
PER SQUARE MILE

1. More than 1000
2. 500~1000
3. 100~500
4. Less than 100

Map B—Connecticut Population.

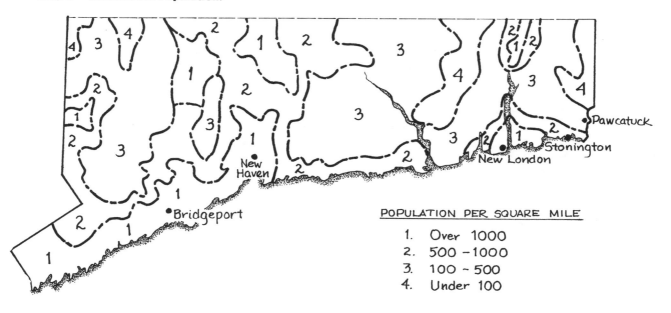

POPULATION PER SQUARE MILE

1. Over 1000
2. 500–1000
3. 100~500
4. Under 100

Map C—Maryland Economics.

Map D—Connecticut Economics.

Map E—Maryland Temperature.

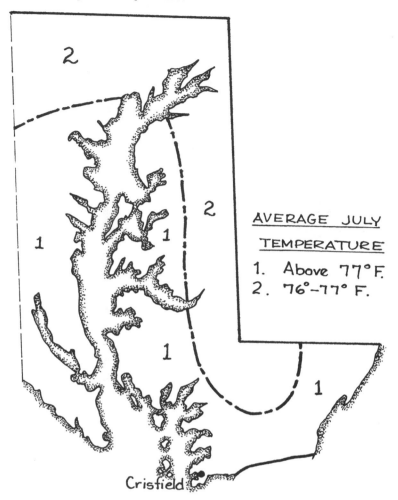

AVERAGE JULY

TEMPERATURE

1. Above 77°F.
2. 76°–77° F.

Map F—Connecticut Temperature.

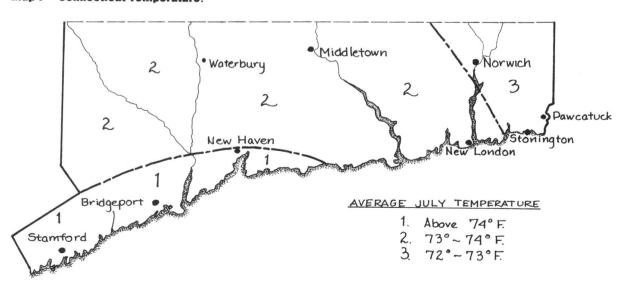

AVERAGE JULY TEMPERATURE

1. Above 74°F.
2. 73°–74° F.
3. 72°–73° F.

Map G—Maryland Rainfall.

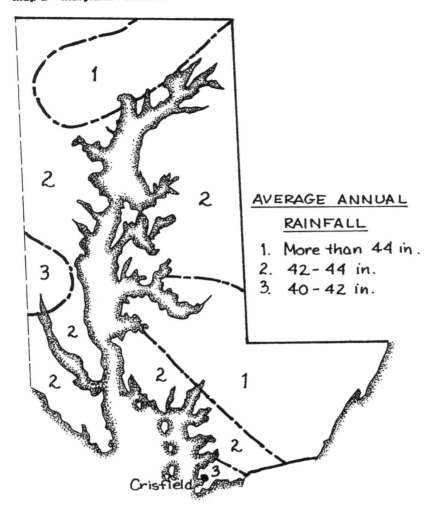

AVERAGE ANNUAL
RAINFALL
1. More than 44 in.
2. 42 - 44 in.
3. 40 - 42 in.

Map H—Connecticut Rainfall.

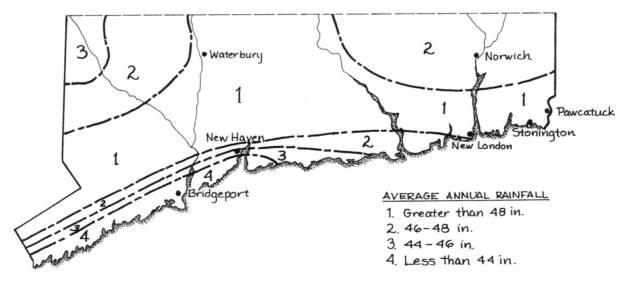

AVERAGE ANNUAL RAINFALL
1. Greater than 48 in.
2. 46 - 48 in.
3. 44 - 46 in.
4. Less than 44 in.

Map I—Maryland Landforms.

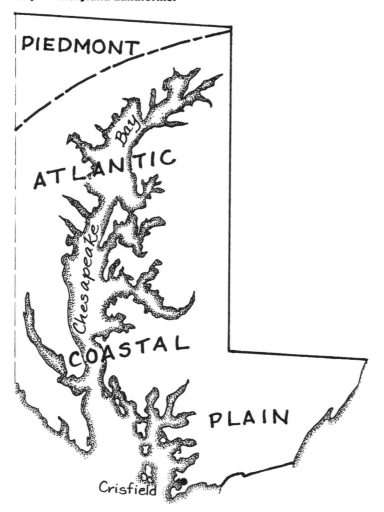

Map J—Connecticut Landforms.

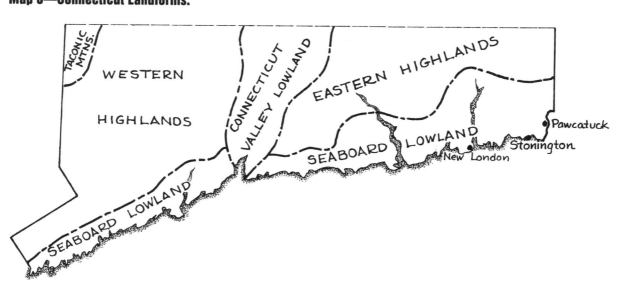

Regional Comparison Chart.

	Bridgeport	Crisfield	Your Area
July Temperature			
Annual Precipitation			
Population Density			
Landforms			
Economy			

B. Imagine that you are going to take a summer vacation in Crisfield. Using the information gathered on the Regional Comparison Chart, what kinds of clothes should you pack and what recreational activities will you plan? Describe the sort of setting you expect to find (busy, urban, crowded, quiet, rural).

C. Now plan a trip to Bridgeport, Connecticut, again considering clothing, activities, and the area you expect to find. Consult a travel guide, encyclopedia, or other reference book to investigate recreational activities available in Bridgeport.

D. Assume the Tillermans have written to say that they are coming to your hometown to visit you. They want to know what to bring, what sort of a place it is, and what they will do for fun while they are there. Write a letter to them answering their questions.

5. Return to the map of the principal products and resources of the Eastern Shore (see maps A through J). Explain how some of these products and resources are reflected in the everyday life of the Tillermans and their friends.

6. Using the information given in part two, chapters 1 and 2 of *Homecoming,* and beginning at the Church Circle, mark the route the Tillermans took through Annapolis on their first day in town on figure 3.16. Locate the spot where they spent two nights.

7. The Eastern Shore of Maryland is located on what is known as the "Delmarva" peninsula.

A. Study a map of the peninsula (see fig. 1.1, Delmarva Pennsylvania) and explain why it was given that name.

B. Apply the same "rule" for naming, and create a name that applies to your home state and at least one adjacent state.

8. Find the following places on the map of Crisfield (see fig. 3.24) and mark their locations in color.

A. The place you think the Tillerman farm might have been
B. The elementary school
C. The middle school

    D. The high school
    E. The library
    F. The fire department
    G. The police station
    H. The hospital
    I. The post office
    J. The airport

9. On a map of your hometown, identify and mark the location of your house and as many of the community services listed in question 8 as possible.

10. Compare the locations of community services in Crisfield and in your hometown. Do you find any similarities? What factors must be considered when locations are planned for new community services like schools, police and fire departments, stores, and libraries?

Discussion Questions

1. In chapter 4 of *Dicey's Song*, Gram says that when she was a girl, Crisfield was the big town, and that people from Salisbury came to Crisfield to shop. What factors led to the decline of Crisfield as a merchandising center?

2. It would be all but impossible for four children to actually complete the journey described in *Homecoming*. Discuss the dangers and obstacles that would prevent such a trip today.

3. Compare the plight of the Tillerman children during their travels to Crisfield in *Homecoming* to the problems faced by homeless people in our cities today. In what ways are their situations similar and in what ways are they different?

For Further Reading

Other Books by Cynthia Voigt

Building Blocks. New York: Atheneum, 1984. 128 pages.
    Brann Connell is sick and tired of the way his parents argue constantly. He has little patience with his father, whom he views as passive and unsuccessful. Frustrated, Brann escapes into a building block fort his father has constructed for him and falls asleep. When he awakens, he finds he has traveled back in time, and the sad 10-year-old boy he befriends is actually his father as a child. When he returns to his own time, he has a great respect for the courage and resiliency of his parent.

The Callender Papers. New York: Atheneum, 1983. 214 pages.
    Twelve-year-old Jean Wainwright is an orphan who has been employed by Daniel Theil to organize his dead wife's family papers. The year is 1894, and Jean, who is staying in the comfortable Theil house, is somewhat lonely, because Mr. Theil seems cold and remote. She makes friends with his brother-in-law who lives nearby, not suspecting that danger lurks

there. As Jean reads the Callender papers, she slowly realizes a terrible tragedy has taken place, and she begins to put together the clues that reveal the nature of the mystery as well as its solution. Winner of the Mystery Writers of America Edgar Allan Poe Award, 1984.

David and Jonathon. New York: Scholastic, 1992. 256 pages.

Sixteen-year-old Henry finds that life has changed for his best friend Jonathon when David, Jonathon's older brother, comes home to live. David survived World War II and the Holocaust, but is now guilt-ridden and suicidal. The situation takes a terrible toll on everyone, including Henry.

Glass Mountain. San Diego, CA: Harcourt Brace Jovanovich, 1991. 288 pages.

Although he does not love her, wealthy New York playboy Theo Mondleigh pleases his parents by becoming engaged to "Prune." Meanwhile, his butler has fallen in love with Alexis. At Theo's engagement party it is revealed that Prune and Alexis are one and the same.

Izzy, Willy-Nilly. New York: Atheneum, 1986. 258 pages.

Fifteen-year-old Izzy tells the story of the terrible car accident that caused her to lose one leg and how her life changed as a result. Although her family is loving and supportive, Izzy's friends are less than helpful. In the end, it is Izzy alone that must learn to live with her handicap. Best of the Best Books for Young Adults (American Library Association), 1986.

Jackaroo. New York: Atheneum, 1985. 291 pages.

In a mythical, medieval kingdom there lived Gwyn, an innkeeper's daughter, who was beautiful, clever, and courageous. Everyone knows of the legendary Jackaroo, the masked rider who helps the oppressed and poor, and, when Gwyn comes upon his costume hidden in a secret cupboard, she assumes the role of the swashbuckling hero. She learns, to her dismay, that there has been a long line of Jackaroos who have all paid the price for their moments of adventure, and the would-be Robin Hood must live by society's rules.

On Fortune's Wheel. New York: Atheneum, 1990. 276 pages.

Birlie, an innkeeper's daughter who lives in the Kingdom two generations after Gwyn in *Jackaroo*, tries to stop a thief and instead becomes his passenger on a stolen boat. The thief turns out to be Orien, a young nobleman who is running away from his role as the next ruler of the Kingdom. The two are captured and sold into slavery, Birlie to a good master but Orien to the fatal mines. Always strong and resourceful, Birlie escapes and manages to rescue Orien, and together they rebuild their lives.

Orfe. New York: Atheneum, 1992. 120 pages.

Paralleling the Greek myth of Orpheus and Eurydice, Enny tells the story of her girlhood friend, Orfe, who helped Enny overcome the cruelty of their classmates. Now they have grown up and are reunited. Enny helps Orfe achieve success as a singer, only to discover her friend has a lover, Yuri, who is a drug addict.

Stories About Rosie. New York: Atheneum, 1986. 47 pages.

This story for younger readers tells of an energetic family dog who lives with a family of four. Four funny adventures are told from Rosie's point of view, including encounters with a bat and a deer.

Tell Me If the Lovers Are Losers. New York: Atheneum, 1982. 241 pages.

Three freshmen at a small women's college are thrown together as roommates. They couldn't be more different in background and attitude, but they develop a strong friendship when they organize the freshman volleyball team. A Best Book for Young Adults (American Library Association), 1982.

Tree by Leaf. New York: Atheneum, 1988. 192 pages.

Ever since her father married beneath his station, Clothilde's wealthy grandfather has disliked his daughter-in-law and grandchildren. Now that her father has gone off to fight in World War I, Grandfather has disowned them all. The family moves to an abandoned cottage on a bleak peninsula in Maine to await Father's return from the war, hopeful that he will find a way to end their poverty. When he does come home, he is so badly scarred that he hides, uncommunicative, in the boathouse. It seems the family will be forced to sell the peninsula, which had been left to Clothilde by an eccentric aunt, to have money to survive.

The Vandemark Mummy. New York: Atheneum, 1991. 234 pages.

The Hall family, or at least part of it, has just arrived in Portland, Maine, where Father is a classics professor at Vandemark College. Mother is pursuing her own career in Portland, Oregon, and 12-year-old Phineas and his sister, 14-year-old Althea, are trying to make the best of a bad situation. When a collection of ancient Egyptian artifacts with a real mummy as a centerpiece is donated to the college, Father is named their curator. Threats to the collection begin to mysteriously appear, then the mummy is stolen. Phineas and Althea follow clues, determined to find the perpetrator of the crime, but they must confront real danger first.

Abandoned, Homeless, or Runaway Children (Nonfiction)

Berck, Judith. *No Place to Be: Voices of Homeless Children.* Boston: Houghton Mifflin, 1992. 148 pages.

In their own words and in poems, more than 30 children, ages 9 to 15, explain what it feels like to be deprived of privacy, safety, school, and home.

Hyde, Margaret O. *Foster Care and Adoption.* New York: Franklin Watts, 1982. 90 pages.

This book examines the strengths and weaknesses of the foster care system including the rights of children and of parents. The topic of adoption is also covered, although in less detail. Lists of groups concerned with adoption, foster children, and searches for missing parents and children are included with an extensive bibliography and index.

O'Connor, Karen. *Homeless Children.* San Diego: Lucent Books, 1989. 79 pages.

This book gives a detailed examination of the causes of homelessness in America and suggests ways of solving the problem.

Abandoned, Homeless, or Runaway Children (Fiction)

Byars, Betsy. *The Night Swimmers.* New York: Delacorte Press, 1980. 131 pages.

Their mother is dead and their father, a country-western singer, works nights, so it is up to Retta (named for Loretta Lynn) to be both mother and father to her two younger brothers. She tries hard, providing food, clothing, and entertainment. For a while, everything seems to be working out, but then, somehow, she begins to lose control.

————. *The Two-Thousand Pound Goldfish*. New York: Harper & Row, 1982. 152 pages.

Warren's mother, an underground fugitive in a radical peace group, has been gone for three years. She is unconcerned about her two children, leaving them with their grandmother and seldom contacting them. Lonely Warren retreats into a fantasy world of horror movies and daydreams.

Cleaver, Vera, and Bill Cleaver. *Where the Lilies Bloom*. New York: Lippincott, 1969. 158 pages.

Fourteen-year-old Mary Call Luther, her 10-year-old brother, and their older, developmentally disabled sister are alone after their sharecropper father dies. They keep their situation secret, even burying their father themselves so that they can retain their home and stick together. Mary Call is the rock of the family, and she fights to keep the little family afloat. Followed by *Trial Valley* (Lippincott, 1977).

Cresswell, Helen. *Dear Shrink*. New York: Macmillan, 1982. 186 pages.

When Oliver's botanist parents leave London to study in the Amazon for six months, they leave Oliver and his brother and sister in the care of their mother's old nurse. At first there is little change in their lives, but then old Barty dies, and the three children are farmed out to foster care homes until their parents return. The adventures they encounter over the next four months are sometimes frightening and even occasionally funny.

Fox, Paula. *Monkey Island*. New York: Orchard, 1991. 151 pages.

Eleven-year-old Clay knows that his jobless father is somewhere in the city, but where? His mother, distraught by poverty and homelessness, has wandered away from the welfare shelter. Now Clay is alone in New York City, living among the shadows of the parks and doorways.

Grant, Cynthia. *Keep Laughing*. New York: Atheneum, 1991. 164 pages.

Shep's father, a well-known comedian, ran off in pursuit of his career and left Shep and his mother when Shep was only a baby. Now, he has suddenly returned and wants to make up for all those years of neglect. As Jeff Greene learned in *A Solitary Blue*, Shep soon finds that empty promises and quickly altered plans signal serious adult immaturity.

Grove, Vicki. *Fastest Friend in the West*. New York: Putnam, 1990. 174 pages.

When 12-year-old Lori meets the new girl, Vern, her first impression is "Weird !" But it isn't until they have become good friends that Lori discovers the reason Vern seems peculiar—she is trying to conceal the fact that she and her family have been homeless for over two years.

Hermes, Patricia. *Mama, Let's Dance*. Boston: Little, Brown, 1991. 168 pages.

Mama has run off and left Mary Belle, who is 11, Callie, 7, and Ariel, 16, alone and in poverty. Ariel has a part-time job to help out, but it is Mary Belle who is in charge. Fearing separation, they try to keep their abandonment secret, but when Callie becomes ill, they must accept help.

Holman, Felice. *Secret City, U.S.A.* New York: Scribner's, 1990. 199 pages.

Two boys discover an abandoned house amidst the rubble of the inner city. They clean it up, make repairs, plant a garden, and invite homeless boys to share its shelter. The boys show a tenacious determination to survive under horrifying circumstances.

MacLachlan, Patricia. *Journey*. New York: Delacorte Press, 1991. 83 pages.

Mama just packed up her things and went away, leaving 11-year-old Journey and his older sister, Cat, with Grandma and Grandpa. Journey grieves and blames himself, and his family gently tries to ease his pain. When Grandpa begins a new hobby, taking family photographs, the boy begins to learn that love still exists in his family.

Sachs, Marilyn. *The Bear's House*. New York: Doubleday, 1971. 67 pages.

The kids at school all tease Fran Ellen because she smells bad, and she sucks her thumb. That's all anyone knows about her. What they don't know is that since Daddy left and Mama got "sick in the head," Fran Ellen, her two older sisters, and her brother have been taking care of themselves and Mama, living on the welfare money, and taking turns watching their beautiful little baby sister.

Spinelli, Jerry. *Maniac McGee: A Novel*. Boston: Little, Brown, 1990. 184 pages.

Part tall tale and part modern realistic fiction, this Newbery Award-winning book (1991) is the story of an orphan, Jeffery Lionel Magee, who is tired of living with relatives, so he runs away. He lives by his wits on the streets of a community torn by racial prejudice but manages to impress everyone with his considerable talent and cunning.

Townsend, John Rowe. *Dan Alone*. New York: Lippincott, 1983. 214 pages.

The setting is an industrial city in England and the time is the 1920s. Poor 11-year-old Dan Lunn has been abandoned by his mother, never knew his father, and is unwanted by his relatives. He must either go to the orphanage or run away, so he chooses to run. After living for a while among a band of thieves, Dan finally finds the family of his dreams.

Blue Herons

Brown, Mary Barrett. *Wings Along the Waterway*. New York: Orchard, 1992. 80 pages.

Twenty-one birds of the wetlands are examined here, including the great blue heron and many others of the heron family. There is a discussion of the habitat, life cycle, appearance, and habits of the water birds and the risks they face as wetlands are threatened. Includes a bibliography and index.

Cookbooks Featuring Eastern Shore Recipes

Andrews, Mrs. Lewis R., and Mrs. J. Reaney Kelly, eds. *Maryland's Way*. Annapolis: Hammond-Harwood House, 1966. 372 pages.

This excellent source includes recipes for many dishes described in the Tillerman novels, like crab imperial, oysters, and biscuits, but the type of service suggested is much more formal than they would ever imagine.

Foley, Jean. *The Chesapeake Bay Fish and Fowl Cookbook: A Treasury of Old and New Recipes from Maryland's Eastern Shore*. New York: Macmillan, 1981. 192 pages.

Tanzer, Virginia. *Call It Delmarvelous: How to Talk, Cook, and "Feel to Hum on Thisseer" Delmarva Peninsula*. McLean, VA: EPM Publications, 1983. 172 pages.

Tawes, Helen Avalynne. *My Favorite Maryland Recipes*. New York: Random House, 1964. 173 pages.

The author is the wife of a former Maryland governor, a native of Crisfield.

Folk Music and Guitar

Bryan, Ashley. *All Night, All Day: A Child's First Book of African-American Spirituals*. New York: Atheneum, 1991. 48 pages.

This is a collection of 20 well-known spirituals with piano accompaniments and guitar chords.

Cohen, John, and Mike Seeger, eds. *The New Lost City Ramblers Song Book*. New York: Oak Publications, 1964. 256 pages.

This collection of American folk music contains many songs of the type mentioned in the Tillerman novels and at least one that is repeated frequently, "When First Into This Country a Stranger I Came."

Evans, Roger. *How to Play Guitar: A New Book for Everyone Interested in the Guitar*. New York: St. Martin's Press. 1979. 124 pages.

Here is an easy-to-understand book for the beginner with helpful hints and clear instructions. Different styles of playing are explained with instructions on buying a guitar, how to play from music, and how to play by ear.

Gamse, Albert, ed. *The Best of Folk Music: Book One*. New York: Lewis Music, 1968. 232 pages.

Gathered in this collection of popular folksongs are many of the songs sung by the Tillermans and their friends, including "Amazing Grace," "I Gave My Love a Cherry," "(The) Water Is Wide," and others.

Walther, Tom. *Make Mine Music*. Boston: Little, Brown, 1981. 125 pages.

The theme of this book is that anyone can make music. A number of simple musical instruments are introduced, and directions are given for making and playing them.

Living with Grandmother (Fiction)

Cleaver, Vera, and Bill Cleaver. *Queen of Hearts*. New York: Lippincott, 1978. 158 pages.

Wilma is to stay with her 79-year-old grandmother until a permanent house-keeper/companion can be found. The willful and peppery old woman has suffered a stroke, so she can't continue her proud, independent life. The trouble is, Granny doesn't like any of the candidates for the job—except Wilma.

Yep, Lawrence. *Child of the Owl*. New York: Harper & Row, 1977. 217 pages.

When her gambler father is beaten up and hospitalized, 12-year-old Casey is sent to live with her grandmother in San Francisco's Chinatown. She misses her father and feels like an outsider in the Chinese community. Her grandmother helps her understand her heritage and makes her feel that she is finally at home.

Maryland

Colbert, Judy, and Ed Colbert. *Maryland: Off the Beaten Path*. Chester, CT: Globe Pequot Press, 1990. 151 pages.

This travel guide gives interesting facts about often overlooked places. Places to see and things to do in Eastern Shore villages and towns are described with advice on shopping, dining, and lodging. Crisfield and other Tillerman settings are included.

Kent, Deborah. *America the Beautiful: Maryland*. Chicago: Children's Press, 1990. 144 pages.

Here is an up-to-date survey of the geography, history, government, economy, industry, culture, historic sites, and famous people of Maryland. Illustrated with many colored photos, maps, charts, and graphs.

Lawson, Glenn. *The Last Waterman: A True Story*. Crisfield, MD: Crisfield, 1988. 210 pages.

For 11 generations, the Lawsons have been watermen on Chesapeake Bay, but today that way of life is threatened as humans continue the exploitation and destruction of life within the estuary. This book paints a clear and poignant picture of the history of the Crisfield area and the impact people have had on the ecology of the Bay. A bibliography of related readings, a glossary, and an index are appended.

McClard, Megan. *Harriet Tubman: Slavery and the Underground Railroad*. Englewood Cliffs, NJ: Silver Burdette, 1991. 133 pages.

This biography of the courageous woman who rose from slavery gives an especially vivid description of her childhood and young adult days near Cambridge in Dorchester County, Maryland.

Preston, Dickson J. *Young Frederick Douglass: The Maryland Years*. Baltimore, MD: Johns Hopkins University Press, 1980. 242 pages.

This well-documented and carefully researched biography tells of Douglass's family background and early years in Talbot County and Baltimore. Details of his life from his birth to his escape north and his triumphant return to Maryland many years later are described in this fascinating, informative book.

Warner, William. *Beautiful Swimmers: Watermen, Crabs and the Chesapeake Bay*. Boston: Little, Brown, 1976. 304 pages.

This study of the Chesapeake Bay, the men who make their living harvesting it, and the natural history of the sea life of the Bay takes place over the course of one year. Along the way, the reader will learn much about the workboats used on the Bay, the ecology of the Bay, and the threats posed to the future of the Bay. Throughout the book are numerous references to Crisfield today and in the past, and the last chapter is devoted exclusively to this town that the author swears is like no other on the Bay.

Wilson, Woodrow T. *History of Crisfield and Surrounding Areas on Maryland's Eastern Shore*. Baltimore, MD: Gateway Press, 1977. 405 pages.

Here is Crisfield's story from the earliest days as a tiny farming village in the 1600s to the present. This history is based on original sources and includes many photographs and articles from the *Crisfield Times* from 1889 to 1973. Also included is a section of local poetry that appeared in the *Crisfield Times*.

Sailing

Adkins, Jan. *The Craft of Sail*. New York: Walker, 1973. 64 pages.
   Clear line drawings illustrate the theory and practice of sailing. Especially interesting is the section on navigation and chart reading. Indexed.

Brunet, Mario. *All About Sailing: A Handbook for Juniors*. Woodbury, NY: Barron's Educational Series, 1974. 192 pages.
   Here is vital information for beginning sailors, from the parts of a sailing craft to how to maneuver it, and from meteorology to boat maintenance. There is a chapter on dinghy construction and a glossary of terms.

Burchard, Peter. *Venturing: An Introduction to Sailing*. Boston: Little, Brown, 1986. 138 pages.
   Here the author demonstrates all the steps necessary for getting started in small boat sailing. The book is profusely illustrated with black-and-white photographs as well as a color insert. The book closes with a glossary and index.

De Pauw, Linda Grant. *Seafaring Women*. Boston: Houghton Mifflin, 1982. 246 pages.
   Here are exciting, true tales of women who were pirates, whalers, privateers, traders, or fighters at sea and the stories of present-day female adventurers. The final chapter suggests present and future career opportunities for women who are attracted to the sea for vocation or adventure. There is an extensive bibliography of suggested further readings and an index.

Paulsen, Gary. *Sailing: From Jibs to Jibing*. New York: Messner, 1981. 159 pages.
   In addition to sailing basics, including advice on boat care, equipment, and emergency procedures, the author devotes one chapter to detailing the repair of damaged sailboats, much as Dicey did with the boat she found in Gram's barn. A bibliography, glossary, and index are included.

Wurmfeld, Hope Herman. *Boatbuilder*. New York: Macmillan, 1988. unpaged.
   The painstaking process of constructing a wooden sailboat is carefully documented in dozens of photographs and in engaging text. Beginning with the early plans drawn on smooth plywood boards to selecting the tree to serve as the ship's mast, this is a portrait of a dedicated breed of craftsmen following an age-old tradition. A glossary of boating terms is appended.

4

Smith and Tangier Islands in Chesapeake Bay

The Setting for Katherine Paterson's

Jacob Have I Loved
Crowell, 1980. 244 pages.

Book Summary

There have been Bradshaws living on the island of Rass in Chesapeake Bay for over 200 years. The small island has diminished in size over the course of those years as tides and hurricanes have worn away the "fast land," turning it into marsh or immersing it forever. But island men still gain their living from the sea, harvesting oysters, fish, and crab. They are called watermen, and Truitt Bradshaw is a waterman.

The story begins during the summer of 1941, when Louise Bradshaw and her twin sister, Caroline, are 13. Their age and parents are all the two girls have in common. Caroline is beautiful, fragile, fair, and musically gifted. Louise, years ago nicknamed "Wheeze" by her sister, is dark, tall, large-boned, plain, and without any obvious talents. It is through the eyes and words of Louise that the story unfolds.

Her mother, who was not born on Rass, had been the island's schoolteacher before her marriage. Now she patiently cares for her daughters; her work-worn husband, Truitt; and his childish, Bible-spouting mother who lives with them and is eaten up with jealousy and religious fanaticism. The island tradition of strict Methodism governs much of family life.

Although Wheeze is only a few minutes older than Caroline, the younger sister is pampered and adored by everyone in the family and on the island, except Wheeze. Caroline almost died at birth and has been considered fragile all her life. Sturdy Wheeze's health has never given anyone a minute's worry, and she mistakenly feels that she is a misfit who is largely ignored. She is secretly jealous of the time and attention her beloved mother devotes to Caroline.

The islanders are isolated from the mainland by miles of water. Their only connecting links to the rest of the world are the ferry that travels daily back and forth to the Maryland town of Crisfield, the magazines and newspapers that are always a little behind the times, and the radio. Caroline, however, has frequent access to the outside world, for she and her mother make weekly trips to the college at Salisbury. There, Caroline takes voice lessons from the head of the music department, who does not charge his talented student the usual fee for private instruction.

While Caroline thrills the islanders as she practices her voice and piano lessons daily, Wheeze prongs for crab with her friend Call Purnell, a fat, nearsighted boy who is a year older than she and is also an outcast. The Bradshaws, always pressed for money, welcome the extra income that Wheeze is able to contribute through her small crabbing operation.

For all her stolid exterior, Wheeze is a romantic inside, and when World War II begins, it provides ample fuel for her imagination. A strange old man arrives on the island, taking up residence in an abandoned house on an isolated spit of fast land. Wheeze immediately decides that he is a spy and persuades a reluctant Call to spy on him with her. Instead, they become friends of the man they call "the Captain," who reveals that he is Hiram Wallace, who left the island 50 years earlier.

Torn by her growing hatred of her sister and her feelings of rejection by her family, Louise begins to hide part of her earnings to save for the tuition at a mainland boarding school. When she discovers that old Auntie Braxton has had a stroke, Louise, the Captain, and Call take the old woman to a hospital and then begin the monumental task of cleaning up her long-neglected house and disposing of her 16 cats. To Louise's chagrin, the charming Caroline steps in to help and captivates both Call and the Captain.

A hurricane hits the island, destroying boats, houses, and land. The Captain has taken refuge with the Bradshaws and, upon discovering that his home and the land on which it stood have disappeared under the water, is persuaded to stay a while, in spite of the noisy objections of Grandma, who considers him a devil. Louise is shaken when she discovers that she is physically attracted to the Captain and horrified when Grandma suspects her secret and taunts her.

Thankfully, the Captain decides to move into Auntie Braxton's empty house. But, when he also decides to marry the old woman so that he can remain there and care for her when she returns from the hospital, Louise is miserable.

Times are hard for the Bradshaws and even Caroline's free music lessons, a financial burden because of the cost of transportation, must be given up. Later that year, Trudie Braxton dies and the Captain decides to use her legacy to send Caroline to a music boarding school in Baltimore. It is Grandma, with her obsession about the horrors of sex and sin, who suggests to Louise the parallel to the Biblical story of Jacob and Esau in which the eldest twin is despised and the youngest loved by God. Louise is in despair, stops praying and attending church services, and feels she has been hated by God without cause since before she was born.

Caroline leaves for Baltimore, Call joins the Navy, and Louise quits school to help her father on his boat. Her mother insists on teaching her at home so that she can finish high school, and Louise passes the high school equivalency exam with the highest score ever recorded on Rass.

Caroline graduates in Baltimore and is given a full scholarship to the Juilliard School of Music in New York. When the war ends, Louise awaits Call's return, hoping he will turn out to be the man for her. It is a cruel blow when he does return and announces that he has seen Caroline in New York and that they plan to be married at Christmas.

Louise decides not to attend the wedding, and instead offers to stay home and care for Grandma. Grandma confides in Louise her own girlhood passion for Hiram Wallace. Surprised, Louise invites the Captain to join them for Christmas dinner and they have a pleasant time together. The Captain suggests to Louise that she make plans for her own future. Having observed in her grandmother the terrible effect limited island life can have on a woman, Louise is willing to consider alternatives.

She discusses the possibility of college with her parents when they return from New York. When her mother reveals that it is Louise she will miss and not Caroline, Louise feels released from the burden of jealousy at last and is ready to face her future away from Rass.

She attends the state university on a scholarship, intending to become a doctor. Instead, she is told she must go into nursing as girls are not welcome in the pre-med curriculum at the time. She transfers to the University of Kentucky, graduates as a nurse-midwife, and accepts an assignment as the only medical professional in an isolated, mountain community in the Appalachians called Truitt.

Filling the role of a doctor for the people of the scarcely populated area, Louise is busy and fulfilled. She marries a widower with three small children, a man who, like her father, is in tune with nature. They have a son of their own whom she names Truitt, after her father. When, on a cold and snowy night, Louise is confronted by the difficult delivery of twins, she is able to save both of them, even the weak one. Her expressed concern to the young parents that both children be loved equally leads to the final resolution of the story as she walks home alone under a star-filled sky. Louise is restored to wholeness when she is able to erase her conception of herself as Esau, hated by God.

About the Author

Katherine Paterson says her primary qualification for being an author is that she was once "a weird little kid."[1] Such children, she says, may retreat into a world of books, and may create fantasies for excitement. She experienced a difficult childhood, feeling she was a disenfranchised outcast.

Katherine Womeldorf was born October 21, 1932, in Qing Jiang, Jiangsu, China. She was the middle child of five of missionary parents. The family lived in a school complex where all of the neighbors were Chinese, and she grew up bilingual. As she got older, she felt that Oriental people had an extraordinary sense of beauty she could only appreciate but never duplicate.

China was in upheaval, and, when Katherine was five, the family moved to the United States. They returned to China the following year and lived in the British sector of Shanghai. Because she heard only English, Katherine's Chinese fluency was lost. Between the ages of 5 and 18, Katherine's family moved more than 15 times, and she found herself in strange schools where she felt like an outsider. It was during this time that she began reading and writing stories for escape and as a comfort.

At the age of nine, Katherine went to Calvin H. Wiley School in Winston-Salem, North Carolina, and experienced the worst chapter in her sad childhood. Small and shy, she was markedly different. She spoke differently and, in her ill-fitting, second-hand missionary clothes, looked like nothing her schoolmates had seen. It was during World War II, and Katherine's family had just returned from China, but the other children suspected that she was a Japanese spy. Tormented and lonely, Katherine found escape in the school library where she discovered the world of children's literature, and found a place where she belonged and was welcomed. She worked as a student library aide, shelving books, filing cards, and helping younger children. She attributes her survival and growth during that most difficult period to a supportive librarian.

Katherine attended King College in Bristol, Tennessee. She then enrolled in graduate school at the Presbyterian School of Christian Education in Richmond, Virginia, and received a master's degree in English Bible. In 1957, Katherine went to Japan, and studied Japanese at a language school and then worked for two years as a Christian Education Assistant for a group of 11 pastors. In 1961, Katherine accepted a fellowship at Union Theological Seminary in New York, where she met Presbyterian minister, John Barstow Paterson. They married and Katherine earned the degree of M.R.E. Their first son, John Jr., was born in 1964, and, six months later, Lin, who had been born in Hong Kong in 1962, joined the family. Another son, David, was born in 1966, and Mary, born on an Apache reservation in Arizona, became a member of the family in August of the same year.

Katherine began writing in earnest in 1964, her first novel, *Sign of the Chrysanthemum,* which drew on her interest in Japan, wasn't published until 1973. This was followed by two more novels set in feudal Japan.

For many years, the family lived in Tacoma Park, Maryland. In 1977, they moved to Norfolk, Virginia. There, her son's best friend was struck by lightning and killed. The tragedy inspired *Bridge to Terabithia,* which won the Newbery Medal in 1978. This was followed by *The Great Gilly Hopkins* in 1978, and *Jacob Have I Loved* in 1980, which won the Newbery in 1981.

Katherine Paterson and her family live in Barre, Vermont.

Setting: Smith and Tangier Islands

Figure 4.1. East central Bay area showing Crisfield, Tangier, and Smith Islands.

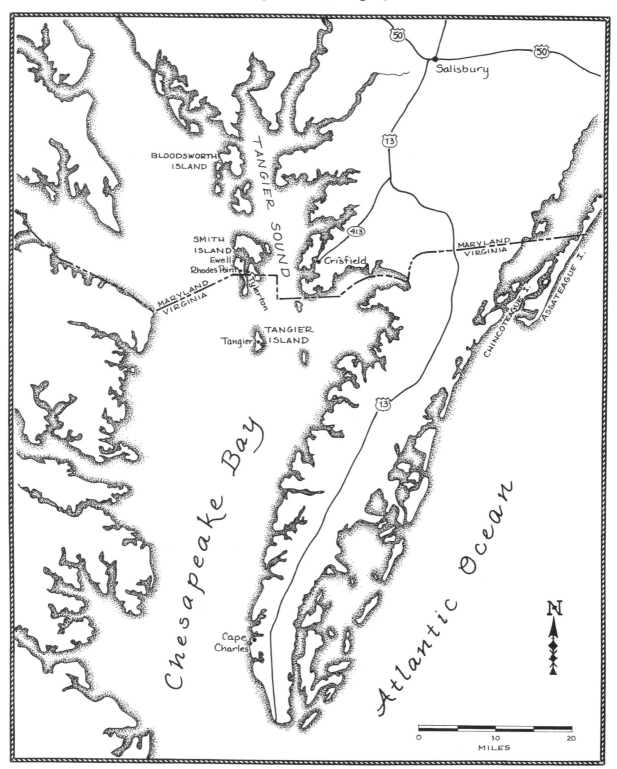

In her Newbery Award acceptance speech in 1981, Katherine Paterson says that the setting for *Jacob Have I Loved* was inspired by William Warner's *Beautiful Swimmers: Watermen, Crabs and the Chesapeake Bay*. She tells how she learned about the many islands in the Bay, most of which are uninhabited. Today, the people of Smith and Tangier islands, although linked to the mainland by telephone and television, still seem isolated from the rest of America. Paterson's story about a young teenager who feels alone is reinforced by the island setting with its sense of isolation. She chose the name of Rass for her fictional island, which is an imaginative blend of many real islands. Both Smith and Tangier have areas reflected in the descriptions of the island that was Wheeze's home.

Tangier Island, Virginia

Figure 4.2. Tangier Island.

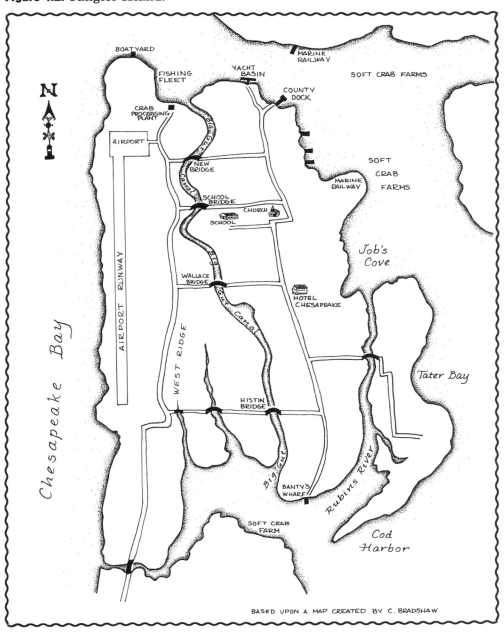

BASED UPON A MAP CREATED BY C. BRADSHAW

Tangier Island is 14 miles southwest of Crisfield, Maryland, but lies just south of the Virginia state line. Tangier is 3.5 miles long, less than one mile wide, and only seven feet above sea level, so that as you approach the village from the sea, the buildings like the church and water tower appear at first to float on the water (see fig. 4.3).

Figure 4.3. The water tower and church steeple are the first things visible when approaching the harbor at Tangier Island.

A cruise ship designed to carry 300 passengers makes the 1 hour, 15 minute trip from Crisfield every day at 12:30 P.M., and returns to Crisfield at 4:00 P.M. Another cruise ship travels from Reedville, Virginia, on the western mainland shore. That trip takes 1 hour, 30 minutes. It is possible to make the trip faster in the smaller mailboat (see fig. 4.4, page 122).

The present population of the island is 659. There is no large industry on Tangier Island; the principal source of income is crab, fish, oysters, and clams (see fig. 4.5, page 122). Recently, an increasing source of revenue comes from tourists who arrive with the cruise ships and crowd into the Chesapeake House for lunches of crabcakes, clam fritters, potato salad, and biscuits prepared by island women.

Figure 4.4. When the mailboat arrives at the dock, townsfolk gather to claim their packages and greet the passengers. A similar scene is described in *Jacob Have I Loved*.

Figure 4.5. Watermen erect crab shacks on the docks for storage and packing crabs. Tied alongside are the boats, with their small cabins in the front; wide washboards; and spare crab pots.

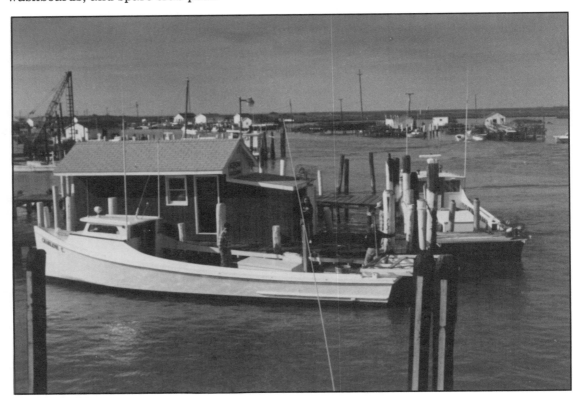

Figure 4.6. This state marker gives some high points in Tangier Island history.

Long before Captain John Smith landed on the island in 1608 (see fig. 4.6), Native Americans summered there, and it is not uncommon to find arrowheads and stone axeheads washed up on the beach after a storm. The origin of the island's name is unclear, but it is known that Captain Smith was a captive in the North African city of the same name. On early charts, the island chain that includes Tangier and Smith islands is referred to as "The Russell Islands." Russell was the doctor on board Smith's ship who saved the explorer who was wounded by a stingray in local waters. It isn't until 1713 that the first record of the name "Tangier" appears.

In 1666, a man named West bought the entire island from the Pocomoke tribe for two overcoats. The island's only inhabitants were cattle and other domestic animals until John Crockett and his family moved there in 1686. The island prospered, and the population grew until, by 1800, there were nearly 100 inhabitants.

In *Jacob Have I Loved*, Louise Bradshaw says that her family has lived on Rass for over 200 years, placing their arrival in this period of early settlement. The name Bradshaw is a common one on both Tangier and Smith Islands, held by prominent, respected citizens. Crockett, Evans, Parks, Dize, and Pruitt are also common names on both islands.

Local legend has it that the first Bible to arrive on Tangier was given to Thomas Crockett in 1775 by two island visitors who appreciated his kindness to them. The book had a tremendous impact, as people came from all over the island to gaze at it and listen as Tom read aloud from it.

In 1780, a little boy named Joshua Thomas arrived on the island with his young, widowed mother. He grew up on Tangier and later moved to Smith Island where he worked and married. In 1805, Joshua attended a Methodist camp meeting near Crisfield and was converted. He moved back to Tangier and became famous for conducting camp meetings that were, at times, attended by thousands of people who came from the mainland. The meetings were held in a grove of trees on the southeast tip of the island. Thomas traveled and preached up and down the Chesapeake Bay in his small boat, the *Methodist,* and became known as "Parson of the Islands." His effect on the local culture is still evident.

Figure 4.7. Centrally located on the island and central to the lives of the islanders is the Methodist Church built in 1899.

Louise tells of Sunday school and Sunday services at the Methodist church. Today, visitors are still welcome to attend services on Sundays at 9 A.M., 11 A.M., and 7 P.M., and on Wednesdays at 7 P.M.

During the War of 1812, Tangier was held by British troops, who used it as a base of operations for their attack on Fort McHenry in Baltimore, Maryland. Up to 14,000 troops were quartered there and two forts were erected. After their defeat, the British troops buried their dead, bound up their wounds, and repaired their ships at Tangier before returning to England. The site of their camp and cemetery is now 10 feet under water, a half mile out in the Bay.

The hurricane that destroyed the Captain's home in *Jacob Have I Loved* is typical of the storms that occasionally sweep the islands. In 1821, and again in 1933, hurricanes caused considerable damage, submerging most of the island, including the lower floors of many houses. Louise mentions the storm of '33, but the storm of '43 that she describes is fictional. Hurricane Hazel in 1954, and Donna in 1960, also caused damage on the island.

The Captain frequently mentions the pasture land that surrounded his home when he was a boy. Tangier, at the time of Capt. John Smith's arrival, stood at least six feet higher than it does now, and was almost a mile longer. According to a Coast and Geodetic survey, Tangier, like many Chesapeake Bay islands, is settling about 20 inches per century. Waves have eroded loose soil and trees have fallen into the Bay. As a result, more earth is carried away until only isolated pieces of marsh remain. By the early part of this century, fields on the western side of the island had become marshes, and several small communities had to be abandoned.

This land loss in the Bay has been going on for centuries, but it has accelerated since 1850, according to Stephen Leatherman, a geographer at the University of Maryland and director of the Laboratory for Coastal Research. During the past century, the sea level has risen about six inches worldwide, but on the Chesapeake Bay it has risen one foot. According to Leatherman, the land is sinking as the water is rising. This "subsidence" occurs because of long-term geologic changes and because of human activities that are depleting groundwater reserves for agricultural, industrial, and household use.

Figure 4.8. The Big Gut is a meandering creek that slices through Tangier from end to end, just as the South Gut did in *Jacob Have I Loved*.

Today, Tangier has its own electrical generating station, post office, fire department, airport, and cable TV service. The health center is staffed by a registered nurse, and, in an emergency, patients can be airlifted to a mainland hospital. This is quicker than the boat service used by Auntie Braxton and Caroline in *Jacob Have I Loved*.

Island government consists of a mayor, a five-seat council, and a deputy sheriff. Islanders work hard to make Tangier a good place to raise children. There is very little crime and traffic consists of bicycles, motor scooters, golf carts, and a couple of automobiles, unknown in Louise Bradshaw's day on Rass (see fig. 4.9).

Figure 4.9. This golf cart and bicycle are common modes of transportation on Tangier.

Students in all 12 grades attend the Tangier Island School just as in *Jacob Have I Loved*; children do not have to leave the island for their education (see fig. 4.10). There are usually about 100 students.

Louise's mother planted a fig tree and a loblolly pine on their side of the Gut, and there are still fig trees in the yards on Tangier and Smith Islands today (see fig. 4.11).

Wheeze explains that because land is in such short supply on Rass, people have for generations buried their dead in their front yards. Caskets have been known to emerge from the ground and float around town during the flooding that follows a bad storm.

Islanders are proud of the fact that during World War II, Tangier had the greatest number of men and women in the armed forces, per capita, of any town in the state of Virginia, and possibly the entire United States. There were 133 men and women in service from a population of less than 1,000.

Figure 4.10. Tangier Island School.

Figure 4.11. The town retains the quiet, unsophisticated serenity described on the fictional Rass.

Figure 4.12. Front yard cemeteries on Tangier.

Figure 4.13. Waiting skiffs are tied up near Wallace's Bridge that spans Big Gut.

Smith Island, Maryland

Figure 4.14. Smith Island.

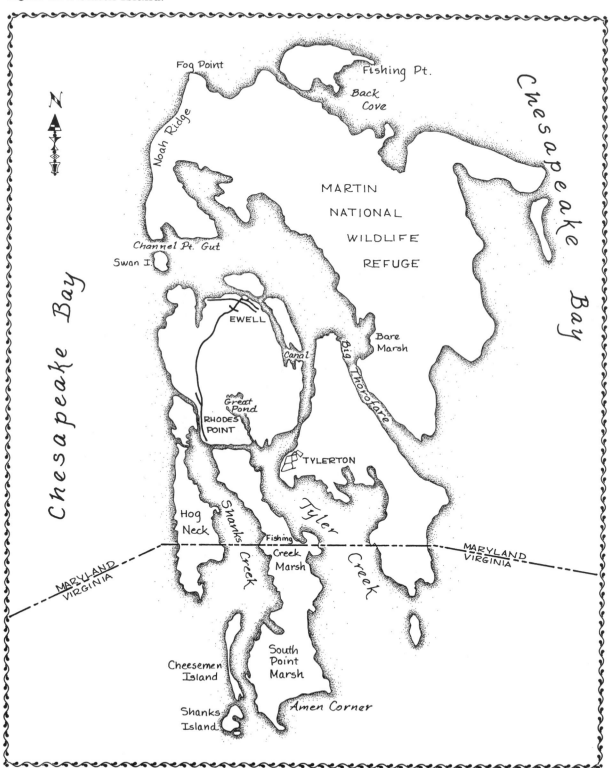

About 12 miles north of Tangier and 12 miles west of Crisfield lies Smith Island. Smith is actually an archipelago, or group of islands, only about 4.5 feet above Bay level and separated by spits, guts, channels, and straits. The whole group of islands is only five miles long and four miles wide and is mostly marsh. North of the islands is the 4,423-acre Martin National Wildlife Refuge in Maryland, but a source of constant controversy for many years has been that the southern tip of Smith lies in Virginia waters.

Figure 4.15. Marshland makes up most of Smith Island.

The population of Smith Island is divided between three villages: Ewell (pop. 300), Tylerton (pop. 145), and Rhodes Point (pop. 200). Like Tangier, Smith was first charted by Captain John Smith in 1608 (see fig. 4.16). The origin of the island's name is uncertain, but it may be either in honor of an early landholder, Henry Smith, or for the explorer who discovered it. The island was settled in 1657 by dissidents from the Jamestown Colony and St. Clement's Island in the Potomac.

Lifestyles are in many ways similar to those on Tangier and the people have often intermarried. Like Tangier, the population was converted to Methodism by the "Parson of the Islands," Joshua Thomas, and camp meetings are still held regularly at Ewell.

Smith Islanders "plant" their dead in the well-kept cemeteries that surround their three Methodist churches (see fig. 4.17). Each grave is covered with a heavy carved stone to keep the caskets from floating into the Bay during a bad storm.

Figure 4.16. This Maryland Historical Society sign gives tourists a brief history of Smith Island.

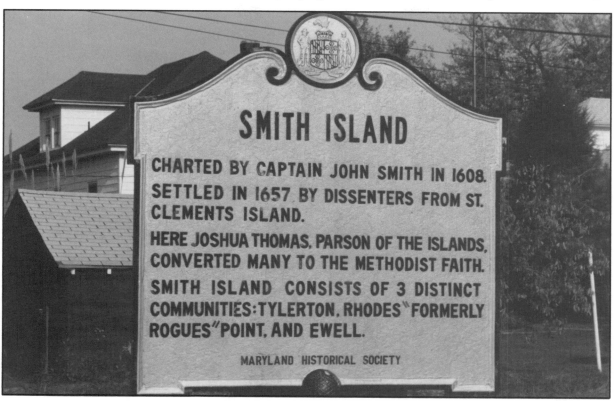

Figure 4.17. Most Smith islanders are Methodists. Each of the three communities on the island have impressive Methodist Church buildings but all are served by one minister. This is the church at Ewell.

As on Tangier, most Smith islanders derive their livelihood from the waters of the Chesapeake Bay (see fig. 4.18). The island fishermen are the champions of the Chesapeake in soft crab production.

Figure 4.18. Docks and fishing boats near the town of Ewell on Smith Island.

There is no local government on Smith Island, and there is little crime. As on Tangier, the islanders are proud of their island and work to make it a good place for children to grow up. There is one road, a mile long, that runs between Ewell and Rhodes Point, and as a result, there are more cars on Smith than on Tangier.

Smith Island is known for its huge cat population. Auntie Braxton would have felt right at home here.

Before 1974, high school students from Smith Island lived with family or friends in Crisfield during the week to attend school. Louise mentions this and saves her money in hopes of attending the Crisfield High School with the Smith Island students. In 1974, the school board contracted a special boat to transport the students daily, from Smith Island to the dock at Crisfield where they are met by a school bus. There are two elementary schools on Smith Island, one at Ewell and one at Tylerton (see fig 4.20, page 134).

For centuries, Chesapeake Bay has offered a seemingly endless supply of seafood and beauty, but today that bounty is under serious threat. Watermen from Tangier and Smith Islands, from Crisfield, and from all along the Eastern Shore are concerned today about the quality of the water in the Bay.

Chesapeake Bay is a rich and productive estuary where salt water from the Atlantic Ocean and fresh water from 48 major rivers and 100 smaller tributaries mix together, creating a rich environment that supports over 2,500 species of plants and animals. But today, many popular fish species exist at a fraction of their earlier numbers because of the loss of underwater grasses essential to life in the Bay. Acres of wetlands are gone. An ever-increasing human population in the 64,000-square-mile watershed basin that feeds the Bay has caused the disappearance of trees and vegetation along the watershed, which, in turn, has damaged the water quality of the Bay.

Algae blooms that deplete water's oxygen are caused by an oversupply of nitrogen and phosphorus in the water. Many aquatic plants and animals require the presence of oxygen. This depletion, and the presence of numerous pollutants, have caused the decline of many species. Today, government agencies, watermen, private foundations, and concerned individuals are working together to save the Bay.

Figure 4.19. A quiet lane in Ewell.

Figure 4.20. The elementary school at Ewell.

Figure 4.21. Seabirds enjoy the view from a Smith Island dock.

For More Information

Crisfield Area Chamber of Commerce
9th Street
P.O. Box 292
Crisfield, MD 21817

Somerset County Library System
11767 Beechwood Street
Princess Anne, MD 21853

Tangier Chamber of Commerce
Tangier Island, VA 23440

For Environmental Information

Chesapeake Bay Foundation
162 Prince George Street
Annapolis, MD 21401

Alliance for Chesapeake Bay
6600 York Road
Baltimore, MD 21212

U.S. Environmental Protection Agency
Chesapeake Bay Program
Communications Office
410 Severn Avenue
Annapolis, MD 21403

Note

1. Katherine Paterson, *Gates of Excellence: On Reading and Writing for Children* (New York: Elsevier/Nelson, 1981): 100.

Extended Activities

1. Use an atlas or a gazetteer to find the "absolute" location of Tangier Island, Virginia. Longitude and latitude will identify the absolute location. The *Britannica Atlas* (Chicago: Encyclopaedia Britannica, 1979) is just one source that gives the absolute location for most cities and towns in the world. Check the indexes of other atlases in your school or public library. Many will give that information.

2. Give the "relative" location (that is, identify it in both direction and mileage) from Tangier to the following:

   Salisbury, Maryland, where Caroline took music lessons.
   Baltimore, Maryland, where Caroline went to music school. Give this mileage point to point, in a straight line over the Bay.
   Lexington, Kentucky, where Louise graduated from the University of Kentucky. Compute that mileage point to point via Charleston, West Virginia, and Richmond, Virginia.

3. Give the absolute location of your hometown and its location relative to at least three other cities.

4. Louise picked the Kentucky town of Truitt as a place to live because it had the same name as her father. Use a gazetteer such as *Webster's New Geographical Dictionary* (Springfield, MA: Merriam-Webster, 1988) or the index of an atlas such as a *Rand McNally Road Atlas* or *Goode's World Atlas* to determine the following:

   A. Is there a town named Truitt in Kentucky, Maryland, or in Virginia ?
   B. Is there a town named Bradshaw in Kentucky, Maryland, or in Virginia?
   C. Can you find any town in the world that has your first or last name?
   D. Is there any other town anywhere with the same name as your hometown?

Map A—Chesapeake Bay Watershed.

5. The Watershed

   A. List the six states in the Chesapeake Bay watershed (see page 137).
   B. Consult the labeled map of the Chesapeake area on page 137. Identify at least six major rivers that drain into the Bay.
   C. On what major watershed (drainage basin) do you live? Hint: Find the stream or river closest to your home. Trace the route a drop of water in that stream would follow on its way to the sea. The last river to carry that drop of water into the ocean is the major watershed for your area.

6. The Chesapeake Bay is the largest estuary in the United States, but there are many other places where the fresh water from a river mixes with the salt water from the sea. On a map of the United States, locate the estuary that would be closest to the place where you live.

7. On page 66 of *Jacob Have I Loved* (Cromwell, 1980), Louise describes the location of Smith Island relative to Rass.

   A. Given that information, draw Rass on the map on page 119.
   B. In what state is Rass?

Map A—Chesapeake Bay Watershed.

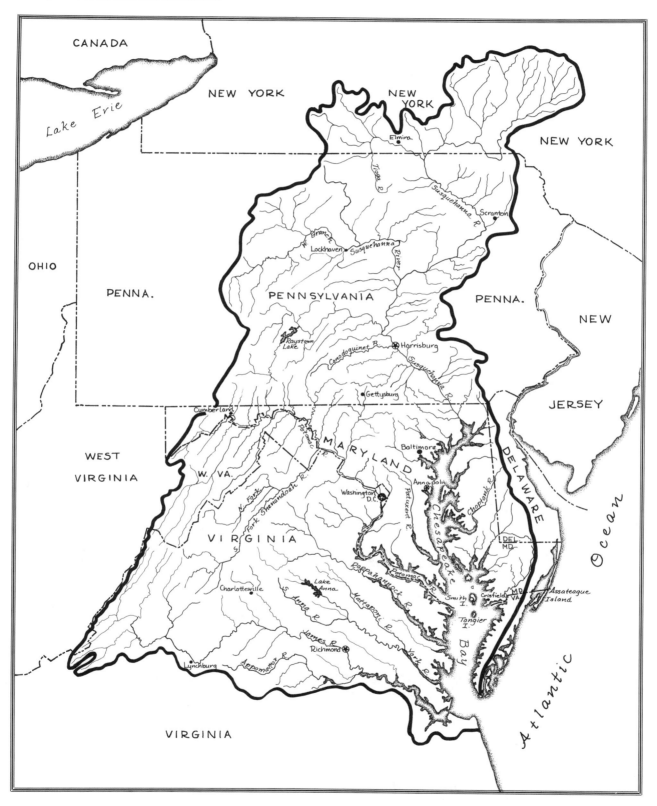

8. Compare the islands of Rass, Smith, and Tangier by filling in the required data on the chart below. Use information given in this chapter and in *Jacob Have I Loved.*

	Rass	Smith	Tangier
Schools			
Location of cemeteries			
Industry			
State			
Religion			
Oyster shell streets			
White picket fences			
Local Government			
Island Ditch or "Gut"			

9. Given the information collected in question 8, does Rass more closely resemble Tangier or Smith Island?

10. The Native American culture in the Bay area is reflected in several area place names. For example, the word *Chesapeake* is derived from the Indian word *Tschiswapeki,* meaning "great shellfish bay." The Annemessex River, located near Crisfield, gets its name from the Native American word that means "bountiful waters." Study a map of your county and try to locate words that have a Native American derivation. Visit a school or public library and consult a book of local history or Indian language to find the meaning of the words.

Discussion Questions

1. For many years, Maryland watermen have been concerned about the fishing restrictions placed upon them by the state government. These restrictions include the types of boats and gear they can use, the times of year they can work, and the species of fish they can catch. Many watermen consider water pollution to be a bigger threat to the animals of the Bay than overfishing. Further discord is created because of the differences in state laws governing the watermen in Virginia and those in Maryland.

   Discuss other industries where environmental concerns seem to threaten the livelihood of a local workforce.

2. When Europeans arrived in the Bay area, it was much different than it is today. In what ways have people impacted the area where you live and what types of action, if any, do you think need to be taken to restore the land and water?

3. Discuss the advice given to Louise to withdraw from the University program for doctors and enroll in a nursing program instead. What factors led to that advice? Now, 40 years later, would the same recommendation be made by a university?

For Further Reading

Other Books by Katherine Paterson

Angels and Other Strangers. New York: Crowell, 1979. 118 pages.
   Here are nine short stories built around a Christmas theme written throughout the course of the ministry of Paterson's husband at the Tacoma Park Presbyterian Church in Maryland. They were read aloud by Rev. Paterson to his congregation on Christmas Eve.

Bridge to Terabithia. New York: Crowell, 1977. 128 pages.
   Jess, a quiet, introspective farm boy with traditional values, practices to become the fastest runner in the fifth grade. But when fall comes he loses first place to his new neighbor, Leslie, an intelligent and imaginative girl with liberal ideas. They become fast friends and Leslie introduces Jess to beauty and sensitivity. Then Jess experiences a deep loss. Winner, Newbery Medal, 1978. ALA Notable Children's Books 1977. School Library Journal Best Book of 1977. Lewis Carroll Shelf Award, 1978.

Come Sing, Jimmy Jo. New York: Dutton, 1985. 224 pages.
   James has been raised by his grandmother in the country while his parents travel, performing in the family bluegrass band. When the family decides he should join them in the singing group, James becomes Jimmy Jo, moves to the city, and is a star. Adjustments are difficult, and at first James hates his new life and his "gift."

The Great Gilly Hopkins. New York: Crowell, 1978. 148 pages.
   Gilly, 11, is hostile, manipulative, and very smart. She has been abandoned by her mother, "a flower child gone to seed," and her current foster parent is fat and untidy Maime Trotter, whom Gilly is determined to hate. Winner, National Book Award, Children's Literature, 1979. Newbery Honor Book, 1979. Christopher Award, 1979. ALA Notable Children's Books 1978. School Library Journal Best Book of 1978.

The King's Equal. New York: HarperCollins, 1992. 64 pages.
   Written in the style of a traditional fairy tale, this story tells of a search to find a princess who will equal the king in comeliness, intelligence, and wealth.

Lyddie. New York: Lodestar, 1991. 182 pages.
   During the winter of 1843, Lyddie and her brother are left alone when their mother takes the little ones and leaves. Later, the farm is let to a neighbor and the two children are hired out. Lyddie is determined to find a new life for herself, so she becomes a factory girl in Lowell, Massachusetts, and endures illness, cruelty, and exhausting work to earn enough money to pay off the debt on the family farm.

The Master Puppeteer. New York: Crowell, 1975. 179 pages.

Set in Japan several hundred years ago, this is a mystery about Saburo, a bandit who robs the rich and gives to the poor, and about Jiro, who has run away from home to work for the puppeteer. Jiro uncovers a dark secret. Winner, National Book Award, Children's Literature, 1977. ALA Notable Children's Books 1976. School Library Journal Best Book of Spring, 1976.

Of Nightingales That Weep. New York: Crowell, 1974. 170 pages.

Takiko is a lady-in-waiting to Princess Aoi in war-torn, feudal Japan when she falls in love with a warrior from a rival clan. This is an historical romance in which Takiko's life is unalterably changed when a dwarf named Goro marries her widowed mother. ALA Notable Children's Books 1974.

Park's Quest. New York: Crowell, 1989. 160 pages.

Park's father was killed in Vietnam and that is all he knows about him. When Park's mother refuses to reveal any history, he sets out to discover what he can on his own. What he finds is not at all what he expected.

Rebels of the Heavenly Kingdom. New York: Dutton, 1983. 229 pages.

Set in nineteenth-century China, this is the story of Mei Lin, who is sold by her wicked father to the army, and of Wang Lee, the young son of starving peasants, who is kidnapped and carried away by bandits. The two meet when members of the Heavenly Kingdom of Great Peace save Wang Lee at the time of the Taiping Rebellion against the Manchu regime. They are swept into the bloodshed and violence and separated as the battles spread to civilians in the name of peace.

The Sign of the Chrysanthemum. New York: Crowell, 1973. 132 pages.

When his mother dies, a peasant boy sets out for the city to find his long-lost father, a great samurai warrior. His mother has told the boy he will know his father by a small chrysanthemum tattooed on his shoulder.

The Tale of the Mandarin Ducks. New York: Lodestar, 1990. unpaged.

In this Japanese folktale, a mandarin drake is captured and separated from his mate by a cruel lord, but is freed by a kitchen maid. The lord falsely accuses Shozo, the chief steward, of freeing the duck and strips him of his rank, assigning him to drudgery in the kitchen. When the maid and Shozo fall in love, they are sentenced to death but are saved at the last minute.

Who Am I? Grand Rapids, MI: Eerdmans, 1992. 77 pages.

Originally written for the Presbyterian Church in the 1960s, this book explores major issues in Christianity, reflected in the difficult world of young adults.

Boats

Adkins, Jan. *Workboats.* New York: Scribner's, 1985. unpaged.

Small craft designed for working off the east coast of the United States and the equipment used for harvesting scallops, lobsters, and clams are examined.

Chesapeake Bay

Markl, Lisa. *Living in Maritime Regions: A Cultural Geography.* New York: Franklin Watts, 1988. 95 pages.
The climate, geography, and cultures of three communities, including one on Chesapeake Bay, are described in this discussion of how coastline resources affect lives.

Warner, William. *Beautiful Swimmers: Watermen, Crabs and the Chesapeake Bay.* Boston: Little, Brown, 1976. 304 pages.
In addition to a fine description of the life of Bay watermen, the current ecological dangers threatening the Bay, and the history of life in and on the Bay, there is a wonderfully descriptive look at real life among the inhabitants of Smith and Tangier Islands.

Wheatley, Harold G. "This is My Island, Tangier." *National Geographic Magazine* 144 (November 1973): 700-725.
This affectionate look at the island is written by a native son who grew up to be the high school principal. His description of returning home after World War II is an interesting tie to *Jacob Have I Loved.*

Wolf, Bernard. *Amazing Grace: Smith Island and the Chesapeake Watermen.* New York: Macmillan, 1986. 76 pages.
Life on Smith Island is accurately and respectfully depicted in interviews and black-and-white photos. The author has captured not only the crabbing activities of the watermen, but the spirit of the people as well. This is a perfect accompaniment to *Jacob Have I Loved.*

Chesapeake Bay (Fiction)

Michener, James A. *The Waterman: Selections from Chesapeake.* New York: Random House, 1979. 193 pages.
These excerpts from the novel weave together the nature lore, commercial fishing, and social customs of the men who make their living on Chesapeake Bay's Eastern Shore.

Sharpe, Susan. *Waterman's Boy.* New York: Bradbury, 1990. 170 pages.
Ben wants to be a waterman like his father, but his father fears that this way of life is disappearing. His mother has just converted their home to a bed and breakfast to bolster their shrinking income. The book addresses current issues of environmental concern surrounding the Bay.

Cookbooks

Available from the J. Millard Tawes Museum
P.O. Box 253
Crisfield, MD 21817

Kitching, Frances. *Mrs. Kitching's Smith Island Cookbook.* Centerville, MD: Tidewater Publications, 1981.

Mother's Favorites from Smith Island PTA. Waverly, IA: G and R. n.d.

Jacob and Esau

The following books have narrative accounts of the Biblical story of Jacob and Esau:

Christie-Murray, David. *The Illustrated Children's Bible.* New York: Grosset and Dunlap, 1982.

De Angeli, Marguerite. *The Old Testament.* New York: Doubleday, 1960.

Horn, Geoffrey. *Bible Stories for Children.* New York: Macmillan, 1980.

Klink, Johanna Louise. *Bible for Children Volume One: The Old Testament With Songs and Plays.* Philadelphia: Westminster, 1967.

Land, Sipke van der. *Stories from the Bible.* Grand Rapids, MI: Eerdmans, 1979.

Seashore Ecology and Environmental Concerns

Bernards, Neal, ed. *The Environmental Crisis: Opposing Viewpoints.* San Diego, CA: Greenhaven Press, 1991. 288 pages.
Articles by scientists, business executives, and environmentalists examine the balance between a safe environment and human needs.

Fine, John Christopher. *Oceans in Peril.* New York: Atheneum, 1987. 141 pages.
The facts of pollution and the implications for our food supply from the sea are presented.

Miller, Christina G. *Coastal Rescue: Preserving Our Seashores.* New York: Atheneum, 1989. 120 pages.
Artificial breakwaters, coastal construction, and pollution have destroyed wildlife and terrain, and an entire ecosystem is threatened.

Parker, Steve. *Seashore.* New York: Knopf, 1989. 63 pages.
The strength of this book is in its wonderful three-dimensional photos that introduce the animals of the seashore.

Pringle, Laurence. *Estuaries: Where Rivers Meet the Sea.* New York: Macmillan, 1973. 55 pages.
Bays and salt marshes are explored in text and black-and-white photos. Plant and animal life above and below the waterline is described. Estuaries are fragile and easily destroyed, and readers will understand why our well-being depends upon their preservation. Chesapeake Bay is often featured in this book.

Rand McNally's Children's Atlas of the Environment. Skokie, IL: Rand McNally, 1991. 79 pages.
Color photos, maps, three-dimensional computer graphics, and diagrams portray the world's ecosystems and environmental concerns. Positive suggestions of what can be done to help preserve them, and explanations of national and worldwide requirements for environmental protection are given.

Sedge, Michael H. *Commercialization of Our Oceans.* New York: Watts, 1987. 128 pages.

This is an examination of the impact of technology on the oceans, focusing on the economic, ecologic, and social problems involved.

Silverstein, Alvin. *Life in a Tidal Pool.* Boston: Little, Brown, 1990. 60 pages.

Information about the struggle for survival of varied forms of shore life is presented.

Tesar, Jenny. *Threatened Oceans.* New York: Facts on File, 1992. 112 pages.

Shows how fishing, dumping, oil spills, and other human influences endanger the ocean ecosystem. Recommends positive actions.

The World's Wild Shores. Washington, DC: National Geographic Society, 1990. 199 pages.

The ecology of seashores in five different climate zones is discussed and illustrated with numerous photographs.

Free or Inexpensive Materials

Alliance for the Chesapeake Bay. *The Bay Book: A Guide to Reducing Water Pollution at Home.* 1991. 32 pages.

How to reduce water pollution through changes in daily life. Single copy free, additional copies are $1 each. Order from: Chesapeake Regional Information Service, P.O. Box 1981, Richmond, VA 23216.

Chesapeake Bay Estuary Program. *The Changing Chesapeake: An Introduction to the Natural History of the Chesapeake Bay for Upper Elementary and Middle School Children.* n.d. 60 pages.

Excellent activities for school and home are the highlight in this well-organized booklet. Available from: U.S. Fish and Wildlife Service, 1825 Virginia Street, Annapolis, MD 21401.

Chesapeake Bay: Introduction to an Ecosystem. Annapolis, MD: U.S. EPA, 1982. 33 pages.

This is an examination of the geology, biological communities, food chain, water composition and fluctuation, and the future of the Chesapeake Bay. Available from: U.S. Environmental Protection Agency, Chesapeake Bay Liaison Office, 410 Severn Avenue, Annapolis, MD 21403.

Twins (Fiction)

Hightower, Florence. *Dreamwold Castle.* Boston: Houghton Mifflin, 1978. 214 pages.

Named a Newbery Honor book in 1979, this is the story of a teenaged girl who makes friends with a schoolmate and her invalid twin brother during the 1950s. Phoebe had been an outcast at her new school until she was befriended by the enchanting Constance Montrell and her charming twin brother, Harry. Soon she finds herself enmeshed in a web of lies and deception.

Pfeffer, Susan Beth. *Rainbows and Fireworks.* New York: Walck, 1973. 131 pages.

The Reisman girls are 16-year-old fraternal twins, but they have always been different, both in personality and interests. Music is Betsy's life, but Meg is a genius at foreign languages. When family circumstances change, the sisters must find a way to get along.

Ryan, Mary E. *My Sister Is Driving Me Crazy*. New York: Simon & Schuster, 1991. 221 pages.

Thirteen-year-old Mattie tells this story of her problems with her identical twin sister, Pru. Mattie is trying hard to be her own person, but she keeps running into a difficulty—Pru.

Vogel, Ilse-Margaret. *My Twin Sister Erica*. New York: Harper & Row, 1976. 54 pages.

Inge is jealous of her twin sister and wishes she were dead. Later, when Erica dies, Inge must deal with her grief and her sense of guilt.

World War II on the Homefront (Fiction)

Greene, Bette. *The Summer of My German Soldier*. New York: Dial, 1973. 230 pages.

In this poignant tragedy, ugly duckling Patty is unable to please her parents, but they love her beautiful sister. Patty makes friends with a German prisoner of war and helps him when he escapes from the Arkansas prison camp near her home. This action causes her to lose everything she loves.

Hahn, Mary Downing. *Stepping on the Cracks*. New York: Clarion, 1991. 216 pages.

Margaret's older brother is overseas fighting in the war against Hitler, and so is Elizabeth's brother. When they discover that Gordy, the sixth-grade bully, is hiding his gentle brother who is a conscientious objector and has deserted the war, they begin to reexamine their feelings about the war.

Lowry, Lois. *Autumn Street*. Boston: Houghton Mifflin, 1980. 188 pages.

Elizabeth is frightened and lonely when her father leaves to fight in World War II, but she finds shelter and comfort in the home of her grandparents on Autumn Street.

The 1940s and '50s

Cairnes, Trevor. *The Twentieth Century*. Minneapolis, MN: Lerner, 1984. 166 pages.

The main themes of this century are presented, including the events surrounding World War II. The focus is on political, social, and technological change. Includes many maps, charts, and diagrams.

Freedman, Russell. *Franklin Delano Roosevelt*. New York: Clarion, 1990. 200 pages.

In well-researched text and innumerable black-and-white photographs, the Roosevelt story is told in the context of his times.

Harris, Nathaniel. *The Forties and Fifties: An Illustrated History in Color, 1946-1959*. London: Macdonald, 1975. 64 pages.

Colorful reproductions of magazine advertising of the era give special insight into postwar Europe and the United States. A chronology of main events, biographical information of important people of the times, and a detailed index make this especially useful.

Wood, Tim, and R. J. Unstead. *The 1940s*. New York: Franklin Watts, 1990. 48 pages.

Science, technology, fashion, popular pastimes, issues, events, and the arts of the 1940s are explored, including World War II and the postwar era in the United States. Includes a biographical reference section and a year-by-year chronology.

Appendix:
Answer Keys for Extended Activities and Discussion Questions

Misty of Chincoteague

Extended Activities Answer Key

1. Map of Chincoteague Island with Circled Locations (page 146).

2. See marked outline map of Delmarva Peninsula (fig. 1.1).

3. A. 1,036 miles
   B. Virginia, Maryland, Delaware, Pennsylvania, Ohio, Indiana, and Illinois.
   C. Answers will vary.

4. Peninsula

5. A. Virginia
   B. Maryland
   C. Wisconsin

6. A. Maryland
   B. Delaware
   C. Virginia
   D. Maryland
   E. Virginia
   F. Maryland

7. U.S. Route 13

8. A. Delaware Bay
   B. Baltimore
   C. Williamsburg
   D. Monticello, home of Thomas Jefferson

9. Answers will vary.

Map of Chincoteague Island.

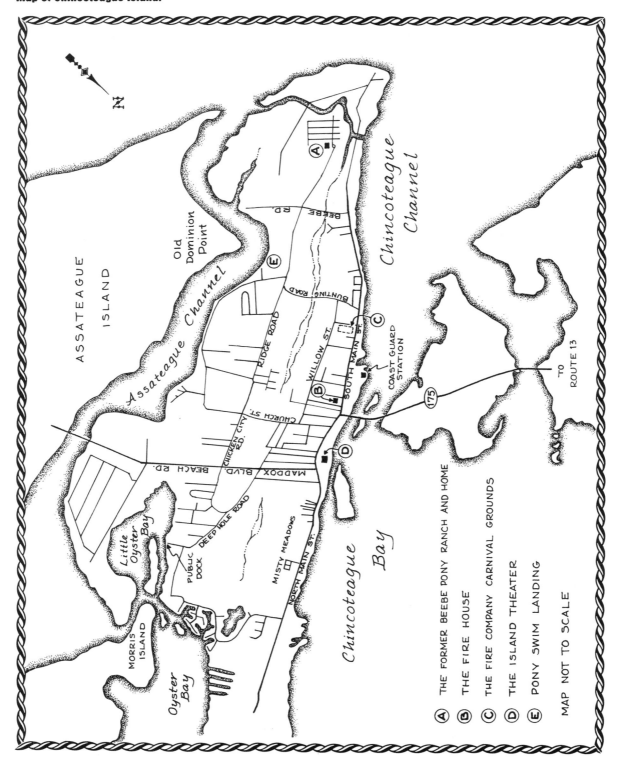

ASSATEAGUE ISLAND

Old Dominion Point

Assateague Channel

Chincoteague Channel

BEEBE RD.

BUNTING ROAD

RIDGE ROAD

WILLOW ST.

SOUTH MAIN ST.

CHURCH ST.

CHICKEN CITY RD.

COAST GUARD STATION

175

TO ROUTE 13

MADDOX BLVD.

BEACH RD.

DEEP HOLE ROAD

MISTY MEADOWS

NORTH MAIN ST.

PUBLIC DOCK

Little Oyster Bay

MORRIS ISLAND

Oyster Bay

Chincoteague Bay

Ⓐ THE FORMER BEEBE PONY RANCH AND HOME

Ⓑ THE FIRE HOUSE

Ⓒ THE FIRE COMPANY CARNIVAL GROUNDS

Ⓓ THE ISLAND THEATER

Ⓔ PONY SWIM LANDING

MAP NOT TO SCALE

The Witch of Blackbird Pond

Extended Activities Answer Key

1. A. 2,225 miles
   B. Barbados is the easternmost island of the Windward Islands of the Lesser Antilles, which are a part of the West Indies. Note: The degree of detail given in the answer will of course depend upon the detail provided in the reference source used.

2. A. Changes from natural causes:

   The channel of the Connecticut River has moved.
   Wright's Island has disappeared.

   B. Man-made changes:

   Streets have been renamed and rerouted.
   Ponds and marshes have been drained.
   Forested areas have been cleared and homes have been built.

3. A. Barbados is in the Atlantic Time Zone while Wethersfield is in the Eastern Time Zone, so Barbados would be one hour ahead of Wethersfield. Note: Standardized time zones were not adopted until 1884, so Kit wouldn't have worried about it anyway.
   B. Answers will vary but should accurately reflect the local time zone.
   C. The answer will be one hour earlier than that given for B above.

4. A. Meeting House=F4
   B. Wharf=D4
   C. Blackbird Pond=H7
   D. The Wood home=E4
   E. Eleazer Kimberly home=G4
   F. Onion fields=F8
   G. Constable's home=J3
   H. The Common=D4

5. Wethersfield Map (page 148)

6. Wethersfield : 41.43'N 72.40'W; Barbados: 13.08'N 59.36'W

7. A. Climograph #1 is Barbados; Climograph #2 is Wethersfield (page 149).
   B. Results will vary.

Key to Question 5

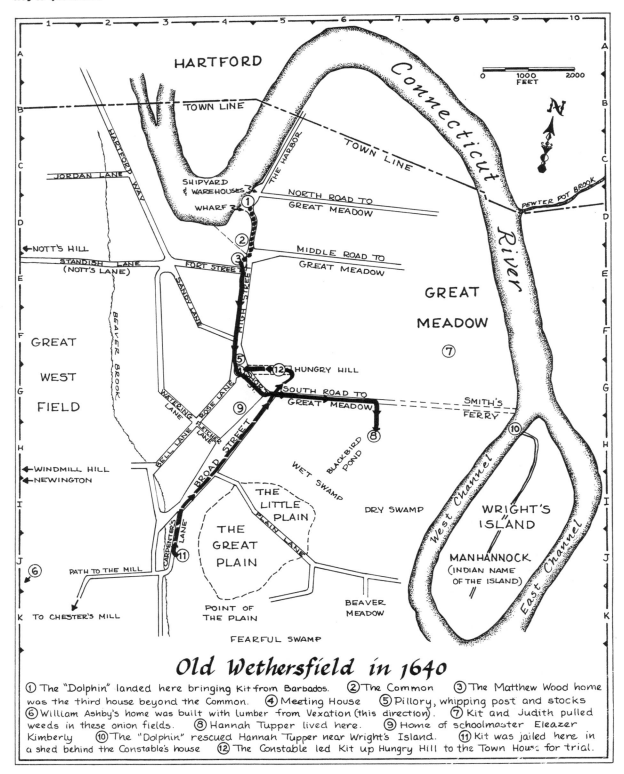

Old Wethersfield in 1640

① The "Dolphin" landed here bringing Kit from Barbados. ② The Common ③ The Matthew Wood home was the third house beyond the Common. ④ Meeting House ⑤ Pillory, whipping post and stocks ⑥ William Ashby's home was built with lumber from Vexation (this direction). ⑦ Kit and Judith pulled weeds in these onion fields. ⑧ Hannah Tupper lived here. ⑨ Home of schoolmaster Eleazer Kimberly ⑩ The "Dolphin" rescued Hannah Tupper near Wright's Island. ⑪ Kit was jailed here in a shed behind the Constable's house ⑫ The Constable led Kit up Hungry Hill to the Town House for trial.

Climograph #2.

CLIMOGRAPH #2
(Teacher's key)

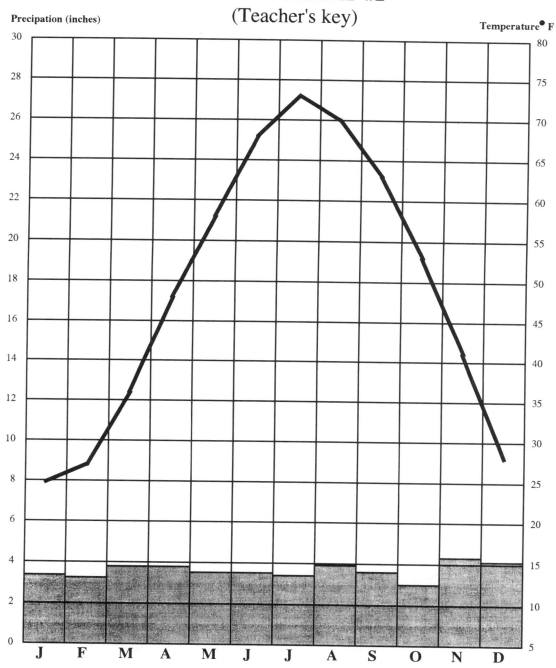

Precipation (inches)

Temperature° F

	J	F	M	A	M	J	J	A	S	O	N	D
Temperature (degs F)	25	27	36	48	58	68	73	70	63	53	41	28
Precipitation (inches)	3.3	3.2	3.8	3.8	3.5	3.5	3.4	3.9	3.6	3.0	4.3	4.1

8.

	In Wethersfield	In Barbados	In Your Town
Crops	Short growing Season, hardy crops	Long growing season, sugar cane	
Clothing	Lightweight for summer, heavy for winter	Lightweight only	
Recreation	Summer and winter sports	Summer sports all year, no winter sports	
Housing	Construction must be sturdy and homes must be insulated	Homes need not be insulated to withstand cold weather	
Energy Use	Heating fuel in winter and air conditioning in summer	Air conditioning in summer	

9. Answers will vary.

10. Answers will vary.

Discussion Questions Answer Key

1. Though answers will vary, some issues that might be considered are the questions of accurately reporting period lifestyles in historical fiction and encouraging an understanding of the attitudes and ideas of the past, as opposed to imposing values and ideals accepted by the majority in our society today on characters from the past.

Homecoming

Extended Activities Answer Key

1. A. The parts of the route traveled on foot were from: Pawcatuck to west of New London in Connecticut, on U.S. Route 1; West of New London to Old Lyme in Connecticut on State Route 156; Saybrook Point, Connecticut, west to U.S. Route 1, then continuing on Route 1 to New Haven, Connecticut; and St. Michaels, Maryland, to Hurlock, Maryland.
   B. The part of the route traveled by bus was from Bridgeport, Connecticut, to Annapolis, Maryland, with stops in New York City and Wilmington, Delaware, and traveling through Baltimore, Maryland.
   C. The parts of the route traveled by automobile were from New Haven to Bridgeport in Connecticut and from Hurlock to Salisbury to Crisfield in Maryland.
   D. The parts of the route traveled by boat were from Old Lyme to Saybrook Point in Connecticut and from Annapolis to St. Michaels in Maryland.

2. A. Miles traveled on foot in Connecticut   74.5

      Miles traveled on foot on Maryland's Eastern Shore   27.0

          Total miles traveled on foot   101.5

B. Miles traveled by bus

      Bridgeport to New York City   58.0

      New York City to Wilmington   130.0

      Wilmington to Annapolis   101.0

          Total miles traveled by bus   289.0

C. Miles traveled by automobile

      New Haven to Bridgeport   22.0

      Hurlock to Crisfield   54.0

          Total miles traveled by automobile   76.0

D. Miles traveled by boat

      Old Lyme to Saybrook Point   2.5

      Annapolis to St. Michaels   35.0

          Total miles traveled by boat   37.5

          Total miles traveled in *Homecoming*   504.0

3. A. Overnight stops were made at:
   1.) An abandoned house near Stonington.
   2.) A small stand of pines off Route 1.
   3.) A house under construction in a development on the east side of the Thames River.
   4.) A picnic shelter on a beach off Route 156 near Crescent Beach.
   5.) Rocky Neck State Park (three nights).
   6.) A creek that fed into the mouth of the Connecticut River, possibly Black Hall Creek.
   7.) A cemetery at Saybrook Point.
   8.) A shaley beach.
   9.) A grove of pines near the entrance to a large estate.
   10.) The entrance to another state park, probably Hammonasset.
   11.) The back of a shopping center where Route 1 crosses Interstate 95.
   12.) A tiny playground beside the Branford River.
   13.) A carwash near New Haven.
   14.) Windy's dormitory room at Yale.

B. 74.5 miles in 14 days of travel is 5.32 miles a day.

C. Answers will vary but should accurately show 5.3 miles from the school.

4. A. Regional Comparison Chart

	Bridgeport	Crisfield	Your Area
July Temperature	Above 74° F	Above 77° F	
Annual Precipitation	Less than 44 inches	40-42 inches	
Population Density	Over 1000 per square mile	Less than 100 per square mile	
Landforms	Seaboard Lowland	Atlantic Coastal Plain	
Economy	Industry	Crabs, Poultry, Corn	

   B. Crisfield is hot and humid in the summer, so lightweight, comfortable, casual clothing would be appropriate. The area is closely tied to the water, with work and recreational activities centered on the Bay. Sailboating, fishing, and crabbing are favorite activities, and trips might be planned to Jane's Island and Assateague National Seashore and Wildlife Refuge. The town is quiet, unhurried, friendly, and very casual.

   C. Bridgeport is a large, busy, industrial city that is one of the biggest financial centers in the Northeast. The climate is somewhat cooler than the Eastern Shore of Maryland and, because it is an urban area, clothing would be less casual than that planned for Crisfield. The activities available include visits to the P. T. Barnum Museum, which features exhibits relating to the show-man's life and times; the Beardsley Zoo; and the Discovery Museum, which contains art displays and interactive science and art exhibits.

   D. Answers will vary but should accurately depict the local setting.

5. The Tillermans catch crabs for food and, in *The Runner, Sons from Afar,* and *Seventeen Against the Dealer,* to generate income. Gram has a large garden where she raises vegetables for family use. The vegetables mentioned are tomatoes and melons, common products of the area. Sammy often mentions raising chickens to sell, but Gram won't consider the idea because she doesn't like chickens. Interestingly, one of the major industries on the Eastern Shore is poultry.

6. Map of the Annapolis historic area with route and Acton Place.

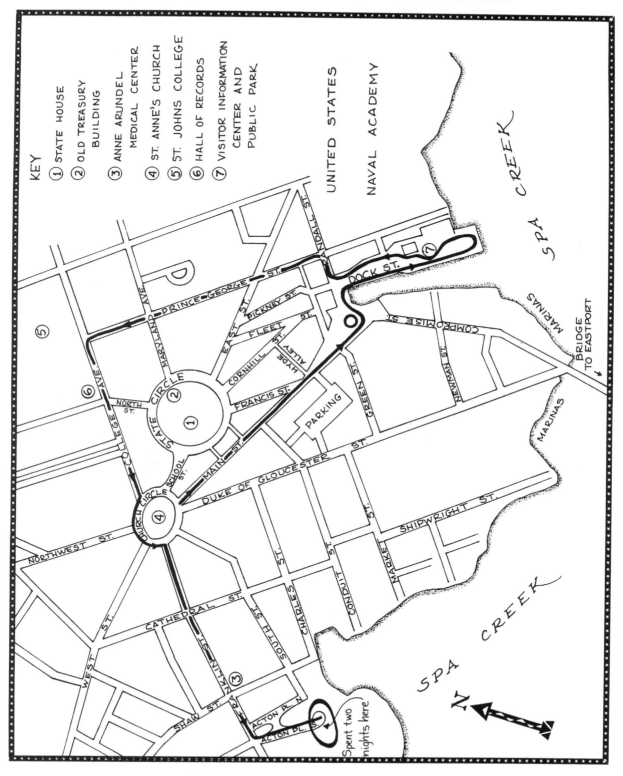

7. A. The name "Delmarva" is a representation of the three states that make up the peninsula, Delaware, Maryland, and Virginia.

   DEL = Delaware
   MAR = Maryland
   VA = Virginia

   B. Answers will vary but the created name should include part of the names of the home state and at least one other adjacent state. For example:

   ARKLOUTEX = Arkansas, Louisiana, Texas
   WYCOLNE = Wyoming, Colorado, Nebraska
   WISMINIO = Wisconsin, Minnesota, Iowa

8. Refer to map key for accuracy (see fig. 3.24).

9. Answers will vary.

10. Factors to be considered vary from service to service. For example, an elementary school should be centrally located, within walking distance from the homes of the majority of students. A library should have access to public transportation, parking, and room for future expansion. A fire department will need to be close to roads that lead to all parts of the area so that it can respond quickly to emergencies.

Discussion Questions Answer Key

1. When the seafood industry suffered a decline, the economic impact was felt by support businesses like retailers, who were often forced to close their shops because of lost business. Buses no longer ran to Crisfield, and the railroad discontinued its service. For those who had depended on the bus and train for transportation, Crisfield became an isolated outpost.

2. In addition to the obvious problems of food and shelter, there are the very real safety hazards that would be faced by children traveling alone and unsupervised today. The danger posed by the evil Mr. Rudyard was but one example of the threats they might face. Illness and injury should also be considered. None of the Tillerman children became sick or injured, other than James's bump on the head, but with repeated and prolonged exposure to the elements and lack of adequate nutrition, it is unlikely that they would all have stayed healthy very long.

3. Answers will vary, but some ideas that might be introduced are the fact that the Tillermans had a definite goal in sight (no matter how unrealistic), and the fact that they were most often in sparsely populated areas where they could camp and be somewhat self-sufficient, maintaining a close family unit. The fact that Dicey was totally selfless and assumed absolute responsibility for her siblings, that she had the qualities of a strong and gifted leader, and that they were incredibly lucky, are also points that should be considered.

Jacob Have I Loved

Extended Activities Answer Key

1. The absolute location of Tangier Island is 37 50' N latitude, 76 00' W longitude.

2. Relative location is

    44 miles southwest of Salisbury, Maryland,
    110 miles southeast of Baltimore, Maryland,
    and about 600 miles northwest of Lexington, Kentucky.

3. Answers will vary.

4. A. No, but there is a Lac a la Truitt in Ontario, Canada.
    B. Yes. Bradshaw, Maryland
    C. Answers will vary.
    D. Answers will vary.

5. A. Maryland, Pennsylvania, New York, Virginia, Delaware, and West Virginia.

    B. Any six of the following:
    Choptank River
    James River
    Nanticoke River
    Patapsco River
    Patuxent River
    Potomac River
    Rappahannock River
    Susquehanna River
    York River

    C. Answers will vary.

6. Answers will vary, but a few major estuaries are Puget Sound in Washington, St. Lawrence River in New York, San Francisco Bay in California, Pamlico Sound in North Carolina, The Hudson River in New Jersey and New York, and the Mississippi River in Texas and Louisiana.

7. A. Rass should be located north of Smith Island.
    B. Maryland

8.

	Rass	Smith	Tangier
Schools	Grades K-12 on island	Grades K-7 on island, 8-12 to Somerset Country	Grades K-12 on island
Location of cemeteries	In front yards of homes	In three churchyards	In yards of homes
Industry	Crabbing, fishing, oystering, and claming for all three islands		
State	Probably MD-Louise attended University of Maryland	Northern part of Maryland, but southern tip in Virginia	Virginia
Religion	Staunchly Methodist for all three islands		
Oyster shell streets	Yes	No	Yes, but recently replaced with hard surface
White picket fences	Yes	No	Yes, but being replaced with chain link
Local government	No police or jail	None	Mayor, a five-seat council, and a deputy sheriff
Island ditch or "Gut"	Yes	No	Yes

9. Rass and Tangier have seven similarities; Rass and Smith have four similarities.

10. Answers will vary.

Discussion Questions Answer Key

1. The lumbering and mining industries are among those impacted by environmental legislation. Students may want to discuss the feelings of the workers in those industries who lose their source of income because of such legislation, and compare that hardship with the hardships and dangers resulting from a threatened environment.

2. Answers will vary, but some possibilities may be the impact on natural habitats, water pollution, air pollution, and erosion.

3. The temper of the times in the 1940s did not encourage women to enter many professions other than those traditionally open to them. The pressure of thousands of returning war veterans, who could now afford a college education under "G.I. Bill" scholarships, forced colleges and universities to take extraordinary measures to accommodate these men to whom the nation felt a debt. Today, antidiscrimination legislation protects the right of all qualified applicants to be considered, regardless of their sex.

Index

About the Author and Illustrator

Joanne Kelly (author) has had an active and avid interest in children's literature since she haunted Chicago's school and public libraries during her childhood. Her previous books, *The Battle of Books, Rebuses for Readers* (in collaboration with Pat Martin and Kay V. Grabow), and *On Location: Settings from Famous Children's Books* have drawn upon her depth of knowledge about good plots, settings, and characters in books for young people, but she has long had an interest in the real places where stories happen. She has a B.S. in elementary education, an M.S. in library science, and a certificate of advanced study in library science, all from the University of Illinois. She has served as an elementary librarian for 24 years and as coordinator of the district libraries of the Urbana School District, Urbana, Illinois for 9 years. When her husband, Chuck, is not taking pictures for Joanne's books, he is occupied as head of Engineering, Office of Instructional Resources, University of Illinois at Urbana-Champaign.

Pat Martin (illustrator) has earned bachelor's and master's degrees from the University of Illinois at Urbana-Champaign and is employed as an art coordinator at Publication Services in Champaign. Previously, during the time that her two children attended Thomas Paine Elementary School in Urbana, Pat volunteered in the library where Joanne Kelly was the librarian. Pat's work at the library provided her with an excellent outlet for her interest in children's literature and art. When her children went on to junior high school, Pat taught undergraduate mathematics at the University of Illinois at Urbana-Champaign, where she served for 7 years. At the same time that Pat began training for a career in graphic arts, Joanne Kelly began writing teacher resource books, which she asked Pat to illustrate. *Newbery Authors* is the fourth book on which they have collaborated.